The Lost Aspect of Love

A book for all adults;

A subject few books discuss;

A tool to enhance all relationships!

The Lost Aspect of Love

Tom Prinz, M.S.
Marriage, Family & Child Counselor

Reed Elliott, M.A., C.C.C.
Speech and Language Specialist

WINEPRESS WP PUBLISHING

Illustrations by Chris Martinez, Ventura, CA

Printed in the United States of America

Packaged by WinePress Publishing, PO Box 1406, Mukilteo, WA 98275. The views expressed or implied in this work do not necessarily reflect those of WinePress Publishing. Ultimate design, content, and editorial accuracy of this work is the responsibility of the author(s).

ISBN 1-57921-098-8
Library of Congress Catalog Card Number: 98-60060

Other books by Tom Prinz, M.S.

Dragon Slaying for Couples
Strengthen and Enrich Your Marriage by Dealing with Hidden Issues

Dragon Slaying for Parents
Removing the Excess Baggage So You Can Be the Parent You Want to Be

To order either book please refer to page 139.

Tom Prinz has dedicated this book to:

Pam
my wife for 30 years, partner in parenting, a role model for me in many ways, and constant encourager. Her encouragement got this book to the publisher.

Robyn, Matt and Chrissy
our three children who now are young adults. You have made your mom and me very proud of you and of the young adults you have become. You have always shown compassion to others! Most importantly we hope that you know that we love you 'no matter what'!

My parents, Al and Esther Prinz
who have consistently modeled showing compassion to friends and relatives.

My clients
who have shared their stories with me; who have openly looked at the lost aspect of love; and who have encouraged me to write this book that many adults need to read.

Reed Elliott has dedicated this book to:

My Dad
from whom I learned the values of duty and responsibility

and
My Mom,
who first showed me the power of sympathy

Table of Contents

Foreword

Today, a deluge of self-help books floods the market. It can be confusing and frustrating trying to decide if it's worth the trouble to read any particular one. I'll bet you're asking yourself right now, "Is this book, *The Lost Aspect of Love*, one that I should bother to read? After all, what is the lost aspect of love, and why should I care?"

Well, the first question is an easy one. The lost aspect of love is *sympathy*. That's right, sympathy.

The second question is not as easy. Like most people, you probably think of yourself as sympathetic. Let's look a little closer. Is your marriage everything you hoped it would be the day you were married? How about your work: are you getting where you want to go? Do others support you and look to you for support? What about your children? It's a rare parent who can honestly say, "Oh, yes! My children are models of sympathy. They know when I'm down, and they're always there for me. They never come around demanding more for doing less."

So all right, already. Maybe life isn't perfect. What does sympathy have to do with it? What are you supposed to do to make life better—take sympathy lessons?

Well, maybe that's not such a bad idea. Honestly now, how much do you really know about giving and receiving sympathy? How much do you know about its effect on relationships? How much do you know about guiding your children into becoming more sympathetic and compassionate adults?

The truth is that most people scarcely give sympathy a second thought. Even books written for professional counselors often treat sympathy as a given, or completely ignore the subject altogether. Far too many people act as if they think sympathy is something a person catches, like a cold or the flu. Either you have it or you don't.

People don't realize that sympathy can be—in fact, *must* be—taught and learned. Because of this, sympathy has become the lost aspect of love. So, we have written this book. There's not a person alive who can't benefit from reading it. Sympathy is a powerful tool that, once learned, can enhance all your relationships—your love relationships, your work relationships, your family relationships . . . everything! This book can put you on the path to finding and using the power of sympathy to change your life. If you only have time to read one self-help book, this is the one for you!

A Challenge

This is a book for those who want to feel closer to others and for those who want more love and joy in life. Anyone who writes a book wants it to have an impact on its readers, of course. Naturally, as writers we want that too. But we want more. We want this book to give you a tool that can change your whole life. You do need to know right from the start that just reading the words won't be enough, though.

In their book, *Days of Healing, Days of Joy*, Earnie Larsen and Carol Larsen Hegarty, quote an old Chinese proverb, "Talk doesn't cook rice." Then they issue this challenge:

> Some of us are crazy about self-help books, inspirational tapes, and personal improvement seminars. We'll buy or sign up for anything, whatever the price, if it promises revolutionary insights or a foolproof new system. We want relief in a day, deliverance in a weekend, and we want the expert of the hour to do all the work for us.
>
> There's nothing wrong with wishing, of course, but there's a lot wrong with kidding ourselves as a way of life. Think about it. If serenity could be bought, we wouldn't need meditation. If personal transformation was simply a matter of collecting enough new ideas, we'd have been transformed long ago. Searching for all the inspiration and wisdom we can find is necessary for growth. But while exploring is great, changing requires doing.

> All the plans and schemes for improvement put together won't change a thing if we don't put the principles into daily practice. Even catchy words are just words unless we accompany them with action.
>
> Today, I will take the best plan I have and put it into action. Today, I will say less and do more.

You'll need to *do* something different if you want your life to *be* different. As you read, remember this challenge.

Introduction

Imagine a doctor trying to operate without a scalpel or a carpenter trying to build a house without a hammer. Even the most skilled professionals would be frustrated quickly without the proper tools to do their jobs. So it is with many adults as they struggle without the tools they need to make good relationships.

Of course, it wouldn't take a good doctor or an experienced carpenter long to realize when an important tool is lacking. Although I don't know much about fixing my car's engine, even I know when I don't have the right tools. Sadly, in human relationships this often isn't true. It's easier simply to blame others when things don't go right rather than ask ourselves if we're lacking needed tools. One essential tool for making good relationships is sympathy.

In my counseling practice, I find that sympathy often is absent in marriages. When partners lack sympathy, many of their interactions are strained and unpleasant. Sadly, they rarely understand why their lives are so unsatisfying. They don't recognize that sympathy is what's missing. This makes the issue even more critical.

Sympathy often is the best tool for resolving problems in marriages and families. Unfortunately, if you lack sympathy, you're likely to deal with problems in destructive ways.

Perhaps you become upset. Maybe you just try to ignore difficult or unpleasant situations, hoping they'll go away. If your children don't do their chores, you may feel that they have disappointed you. Maybe you become angry, blaming and shaming them for their shortcomings. Maybe you simply feel frustrated or betrayed. Perhaps your children are afraid of the dark and you find yourself getting impatient with them, adding guilt to their feelings of fear. In situations like these, new tools, better tools are needed.

Sometimes I try to ignore broken things around my house because I lack tools, or just don't know how to fix what's broken. Unfortunately, when I do this, I find that things just stay broken; they never fix themselves. Similarly, if your relationships are falling apart because you lack tools, or don't know how to fix them, you'll find that ignoring the problems only makes them worse. Relationships don't mend themselves.

If you want to improve your connections with others, you'll need a new tool and you'll have to learn how to use it. That new tool could be sympathy.

We've written this book with the average adult, the average couple, the average parents, in mind. It will help you live and work productively with those who aren't sympathetic. It will teach you how to be sympathetic to yourself. It will help you raise sympathetic and compassionate children. It will teach you how to make your marriage more joyful, and long-lasting.

We believe that this book also can be helpful to counselors and therapists. We encourage them to explore the issues of sympathy in their professional practice. Like many people, counselors tend to assume that "normal" adults already have learned how to be sympathetic. Sympathy is not caught; it must be taught! Let this book be your teacher.

Chapter 1
What Is Sympathy?

The dictionary defines sympathy as, "Having or showing kindness to others; pity or compassion felt for another's suffering; the ability to enter into another person's mental state, feelings, or emotions." Sympathy means more than just understanding how others feel. It means doing something to help them feel better.

One way to understand what sympathy *is*, is to list some examples of what it *is not*. These examples are taken from real stories I have heard in the course of counseling. As you read them, you will see how sympathy, or its lack, may affect your life. You also will begin to understand why I thought a book about sympathy is needed.

- A mother living in Germany didn't call her adult daughter, who lived in California, to tell her that her father had died. Instead, she sent a letter with the newspaper clipping of the father's death notice.
- One man refused to help his wife carry in some heavy sacks of water-softening salt. Instead, she had to empty them using a small pan, carrying the salt, pan by pan, from the car.
- A woman asked her mother, who was living with her, if she would help with dinner. Her mother replied, "Why should I? If I weren't here you'd have to do it yourself."

- A man bought a new car for his wife without consulting her. He bought what he thought she should have, not what she wanted. She hated the car every time she drove it.
- Another man didn't accompany his wife to either of her parents' funerals.
- A father got angry with his son for crying when the father left to go to the store.
- The wife of a pastor said, "You can preach. Don't worry about a little cold." He preached that Sunday, but on Monday required admission to a hospital with a serious illness.
- A husband was upset that his wife would not have sex with him one week after her hysterectomy.
- A man got a vasectomy without his wife's approval. He said it was his body; he could do what he wanted with it. He had forged his wife's name on the doctor's consent form.
- A man sold the family's second car without checking with his wife.
- A mother told her son that he shouldn't be afraid of the dark. She said it was ridiculous to be afraid in their house because the doors were locked and the family dog was there to protect everyone.

Everyone acts unsympathetically sometimes. My wife, Pam, would like to be a professional photographer. I'll never forget the time that a photo she had submitted for a brochure was rejected. Instead of being sympathetic I said, "That's no big deal; thirty publishers rejected my first book."

Perhaps you've seen yourself, or your spouse, in some of these examples. Everyone has experienced incidents where sympathy was missing. This book will help you learn to be more sympathetic, to understand why some people aren't sympathetic, and to teach others to be more sympathetic, both to you and to themselves. Incidents like the ones above no longer need to be a constant part of your life. Instead, you can experience the positive power of sympathy.

Chapter 2

Why Do Some People Have Trouble Being Sympathetic?

To understand why you or your spouse may have trouble being sympathetic, it's important to look at your childhood. Some therapists call this "doing family of origin work." We don't look into the past to find someone to blame for present problems. We look to gain understanding about what may be influencing how we act now.

Most adults fall into one of three categories based on how well they understand the effects of childhood experience on adult feelings and beliefs. Before we go further, let's look at these three categories.

One group blocks out, or has forgotten, most of their childhood. These people have little or no memory of anything that happened to them. They tend to think that childhood issues can't influence them since they don't remember any specifics. To me this seems a little like thinking you won't be hurt if a truck runs over you as long as you don't see it coming.

A second group remembers what happened to them as children. They may even remember how they felt, but they don't feel that their childhood can affect them now. I recall working with one man in counseling who told me that he was too "macho" to be affected by his childhood anymore. How wrong he was! It has been said that those who don't study the past are doomed to repeat it. This is just as true about family histories as it is about national histories. If we don't study and learn from the mistakes made in our childhood families, we almost certainly will repeat them in our adult families.

A final group accurately remembers the painful things that happened to them as children, and how they felt at the time. Further, they believe they already have done the emotional work needed to overcome any negative effects of these experiences. They have stopped thinking about them or working on them. I find that women are more likely than men to fall into this category. Because women often deal with feelings more readily than men do, they are more likely to have worked on remembering childhood pain and understanding how it affects their lives now. Unfortunately, many still struggle with problems in their marriage relationships because they never completed the work needed to overcome the impact of childhood traumas. It's a little like trying to live in a house with no roof. A half-finished house doesn't provide much more shelter than no house at all. We need to keep working until we finish the whole job.

Adults in all three categories continue to be affected in many ways by their childhood. Just because you've forgotten your childhood doesn't mean that it no longer affects you. Just because you've done some work doesn't mean you've finished the job.

Into which of the three categories do you think you fall? Into which category do you think your spouse falls? Talk about this with each other and tell why you feel that you're in a particular category.

Looking back at your childhood can give you considerable insight into your views now. It also can help you see why you use or lack sympathy in your current relationships.

Many adults interpret their spouse's lack of sympathy as a lack of love. I believe that the two things can be separate. Your spouse truly may love you but never have learned the importance of sympathy or how to show it.

If you asked your husband to speak French, he might reply, "Sorry, but I didn't learn it in school." If that was his response, I'm sure you'd understand. In such a case you wouldn't feel badly or tell yourself that he could speak French if he really loved you.

The same applies to sympathy. If your husband didn't learn sympathy as a child, then it's unreasonable to expect him to speak sympathy now. First, he will need to learn this new language and believe in its importance.

I once counseled with a woman who couldn't understand or forgive her parents for playing golf on the day that her three-year-old child had open-heart surgery. Most of us would expect such a moment to bring out a sympathetic response from grandparents, and usually it would. Still, we must remember that being dropped in the middle of France doesn't mean that you would suddenly be able to speak French. You still would have to take some lessons. The same is true for sympathy. Situations won't automatically bring out sympathy in a person who hasn't learned how to be sympathetic.

We all need to look at our past to understand why we act as we do. For most people there is no single, major event that affected them. What's important are the more subtle factors that were present throughout childhood.

Picture a sailboat going across an ocean. It's unlikely that the boat will hit a single iceberg and sink. On the other hand, it's almost certain that the boat will pick up some barnacles. These definitely will slow it down, and may even sink it over time.

So it is when we look at our past. We don't look expecting to find one major event that determined whom we became. Rather, we look hoping to identify the "barnacles" that are slowing us down and holding us back. These "barnacles" are the many seemingly innocent events that affected our lives, especially those that formed our concept of sympathy.

There are many reasons why people may not be sympathetic or may not be able to accept sympathy. Below, I'll list a few. As you read my suggestions, mark the ones that apply to you, and list others that I may have left out. Also, mark those reasons that you feel apply to your spouse. Later, discuss these at a time when your spouse is feeling comfortable and receptive.

- Perhaps your father was not sympathetic to the needs of your mother. Maybe he didn't help with the housework, pick up after himself, or take over some of your mother's jobs when she was sick. A man once told me that if his mother was sick when his father came home, the father would make dinner for himself, but not for his wife and six children. One of my clients told me how his father kept his mother on a very tight budget, though the family had plenty of money.
- Perhaps your mother wasn't sympathetic to your father's needs when he was sick. Maybe she didn't ask him about his work or how he was feeling.
- Maybe your father didn't consult with your mother or with the children about their vacation wishes. He may just have

Many adults heard comments like this when they were growing up. Perhaps such parents were well-meaning, but they gave the message that "It's not okay to cry or even admit there is pain." Because of this, many adults "pretend" when they are in pain and don't give others any opportunity to be sympathetic.

decided where the family should go, and forced everyone else to comply with his decision.

- Perhaps your parents gave you the message that you had no right to cry. Maybe you heard, "Don't cry; it doesn't hurt," or "If you want to cry, I'll give you something to cry about." You may have learned early in life that it didn't do any good to express your feelings, because no one listened or accepted them. One woman told me that her father got mad when she broke her arm at school because he had to leave work to take her to the doctor. Another woman recalled riding in the back of the family truck and falling out because her father was speeding. Her dad said she was fine, but since she was complaining she could ride in the front. A visit to the doctor later revealed several broken bones.
- Perhaps your parents weren't ever home when you returned from school. Nobody was there to discuss your feelings or ask how your day went. You may have learned simply to keep your feelings to yourself. If you were never given sympathy, you may not have experienced how helpful and healing it can be.
- Perhaps you had a mother or father who never admitted being sick or never allowed themselves to complain or express their feelings. In such a case you may not have learned how to show sympathy because you did not get the opportunity to practice.
- You may have had a mother or father who always was sick. One man told me that he could always remember feeling that his father was about to die because of his constant complaints about his health. It didn't take long for him to learn to tune out his father. As an adult, he was indifferent not only to his own health and feelings, but also to the welfare of others.
- Maybe your father was the kind of man who would move the family from city to city without consulting other family members or considering their input important.
- Perhaps you were ignored when you got sick or scared, or didn't like a particular activity. One man told about playing in Little League for eight years at his parents' insistence and hating every minute. He had poor vision and trouble seeing

the ball, but he never dared to speak up to get glasses. To this day he hates baseball.

- Perhaps you grew up with a single parent because of divorce or death. It can be hard to learn sympathy without role models to demonstrate it. For example, it's helpful to have one parent reinforce the need for a child to be sympathetic toward the other parent. If mom is sick, dad can tell the kids to keep the noise down or show them how to make soup for their mom. Without such reinforcement, it's hard to learn to be sympathetic. I have counseled with many children and teenagers in single-parent families and have observed how hard it often is for them to be sympathetic.

Points to Ponder

1. Which of the above situations may have affected your views of sympathy?
2. Which situations describe why your spouse may have difficulty with sympathy?
3. What other factors may have affected your acceptance of the need for sympathy in relationships?

Chapter 3
Survey on Sympathy

We encourage you to complete this survey as a follow-up to the previous chapter. It will help you understand your views on sympathy and give you some answers about why you act the way you do in relationships. Remember, you're looking at your past to gain understanding, not to find fault. Some additional questions are included about the present to help you learn to use the tool of sympathy now. The survey also will prepare you for some sympathy issues we'll discuss later. Write out your answers and give specific examples that support each. After completing the survey, compare your answers to those of your spouse.

1. Was your mother sympathetic to your father?
2. Was your father sympathetic to your mother?
3. Was your mother sympathetic to you?
4. Was your father sympathetic to you?
5. Is your spouse sympathetic to you? If your answer is no, what would you like him or her to do differently?
6. Are you sympathetic to your spouse? Again, if your answer is no, what might you do differently?
7. Are you sympathetic to your children?
8. Do you make it hard for people to be sympathetic to you?
9. Are you sympathetic to yourself?

Chapter 4

What Do People Do Instead of Accepting Sympathy?

Sooner or later everyone goes through difficult and stressful times. Everyone knows how it feels to be depressed or overwhelmed by life. All of us have experienced disappointments, a missed promotion, a defeat in a school election, an invitation that didn't come for some special party. We all must deal with the loss of loved ones, sometimes because of death, sometimes because of divorce or abandonment.

What happens when people don't accept sympathy or don't get sympathy after experiencing such pain? Where do the pain and the sadness go? Where does the frustration go? Where does the anger go?

Such feelings don't disappear; they don't just go away. We may try to ignore them for a while, but eventually we will have to deal with them in some way. If sympathy is missing, that way is likely to be unhealthy and destructive.

When I counsel with young children, I jokingly say that feelings are like little "animals" running around in your stomach. If you don't let them out and deal with them, you'll need to feed them. They will multiply and cause you increasing discomfort.

Physical Pain Can Result When Feelings Are Repressed

Although there are probably as many destructive ways of dealing with pain as there are individual adults, there are some common approaches. Many people simply suppress their feelings, pretending that they feel fine when they're really in terrible pain.

Our body responds to repressed feelings in a variety of ways that depend on the individual. One person may get headaches, another may get an ulcer. Another may break out in a rash. Scientists even have traced some types of cancer to the repression of feelings. There is no question that holding in painful feelings can cause physical problems.

Lashing Out at Others in Anger

Physical symptoms are one result of trying to hold in feelings. Emotional or angry outbursts are another. Repressed pain and grief can cause people to lash out in anger, either verbally or physically. For example, constantly criticizing and complaining are verbal ways of handling emotional pain. Fighting or abusing others are physical ways.

Sometimes we hear of murderers who say that they kill because of bottled-up rage over past mistreatment. Such violence also can be turned inward in the deadly form of suicide. Suicide is a passive-aggressive way of handling anger. It can be an attempt to make loved ones angry. Some people think that when they make others angry, they're hurting them. More often they only hurt themselves, fatally, in the case of suicide.

The Need to Numb the Feelings

The use of drugs, alcohol, and tobacco is common in our society. These all feed those little inside feeling "animals" I mentioned earlier. Substance abuse is a way to keep them happy or at least to keep them quiet. Many adults and teenagers resort to abuse of drugs, alcohol, and tobacco to suppress the pain of disappointments and lost dreams. Similarly, others overeat to ease their pain and to feed the little "animals."

When adults don't share their feelings and accept sympathy, they may tend to handle pain by smoking, drinking, or taking drugs.

Escape Through Books, TV or Sports

Some adults avoid painful feelings or situations by escaping into television. Others read novel after novel, burying themselves in imaginary lives to leave their painful, real feelings temporarily behind. Still others escape by playing sports or following sports excessively.

Don't get me wrong. I enjoy watching television, reading books, and playing and following sports. It's doing these things to excess that signals and causes problems. Such activities can push others away and exclude them. Couples may find themselves sharing less and less. They may become increasingly separate and isolated.

When we handle pain inappropriately, we distance ourselves from those we love. On the contrary, when we handle our feelings in appropriate and healthy ways, others can get closer to us. They can give us the sympathy we need to heal.

Workaholism: the "Ism" That Gets Rewarded

Some adults deal with painful feelings or emotions by burying themselves in work. Always keeping busy makes it easy to ignore painful feelings, temporarily at least. Still, the feelings are there. They are always trying to surface and call attention to themselves.

I once counseled with a woman who was sexually abused by both her brothers. One of her coping strategies was to stay busy, to keep working, always to be doing something. Each week in counseling, as we'd begin to talk about her brothers, the hurt surfaced quickly and the tears flowed.

This woman's feelings were so close to the surface that they readily came out as soon as she began to discuss them. It was easy to feel sympathy for her then, but no one ever gave her sympathy when all they saw was her superficial busyness. She began to receive sympathy, and to heal, when she stopped pretending that the feelings weren't there.

This woman also used another destructive strategy to deal with her repressed feelings—perfectionism.

Perfectionism

Many adults who have been hurt as children make a vow of perfectionism. Unconsciously they think, "If I'm perfect I won't deserve bad things, so nothing bad will happen to me." They spend the rest of their lives trying to be perfect. This has the added advantage of keeping them very busy, so they also avoid having to face painful feelings. Unfortunately, bad things happen even to people who are trying their best to be perfect. Perfectionists have special difficulty dealing with the unavoidable injustices of life. For them, the slightest setback becomes an arrow to the heart, a source of guilt, and a motive to redouble their frantic efforts to be perfect. Dr. David Stoop's book, *Living with a Perfectionist,* is excellent reading for perfectionists and those who live with them.

Unhealthy Vows

There are many kinds of unhealthy vows that adults and children make to deal with unresolved pain. For example, a child whose dog has died may decide, "I'll never get another dog." Some children isolate themselves if others painfully disappoint them, vowing to be alone rather than risk being hurt. Perhaps you made a vow never to get close to anyone again because your mother, father, or other adults hurt you.

These sorts of vows attempt to deal with pain by avoiding all situations that could cause it. Unfortunately, when we make vows like this, we also are avoiding the potential rewards of love and friendship.

Making unhealthy vows is a common way to deal with repressed pain. It also is a destructive way that sets us up for more pain, not less. I recommend Rich Buhler's book, *Pain and Pretending*, for more information about destructive vows.

Affairs

Some adults go outside their marriages for support and sympathy. Many affairs happen because partners do not share painful feelings, frustrations, or disappointments with each other. If a spouse shows no sympathy to the pains and disappointments of his or her mate, the marriage is in trouble.

As children, some people never learn to share feelings within their family. They carry the belief into their marriages that feelings are not a proper part of family life. Such people are unable to share feelings with their spouses. Since they don't know how to get comfort and sympathy in their marriages, they go outside for it.

This also may be a continuation of a childhood strategy. In families where children cannot get sympathy and understanding, they learn to go to friends, classmates, or others outside the family for consolation. They may continue the strategy of going outside the home for support in adulthood and in their marriages.

Reactions to Midlife Issues

During a midlife crisis, some individuals suddenly will want to quit their jobs, buy new cars, or have affairs with younger people. All these can be inappropriate ways to deal with the feelings that accompany midlife times.

Midlife questioning and anxiety is normal. This is a natural time for people to evaluate what they have done in life and to consider what they want to do in the future. In midlife, people must come to grips with a changing body and with children leaving home. It's a time when many people have to grieve the loss of dreams, the loss of ideals about physical appearance, the loss of health, and the loss of their children who now are becoming adults. It's easy to imagine how such major life changes can cause anxiety and depression.

I believe that our society makes too much fun of serious midlife crisis issues. It becomes difficult for adults to handle midlife feelings in healthy and positive ways because they're afraid to admit having the feelings. It's important to discuss and deal appropriately with all the feelings that are associated with midlife issues.

There are many good books about the time of midlife crisis. Jim and Sally Conway have written some of my favorites including, *Men In Midlife Crisis*, *You and Your Husband's Midlife Crisis*, and *Women in Midlife Crisis*.

Points To Ponder:

1. Which ways of handling pain discussed in this chapter have you used or are you using now?
2. Which have you observed your spouse using?
3. Discuss your responses with your spouse.

Chapter 5
Where Is Sympathy Needed in Relationships?

Many books discuss ways to strengthen interpersonal relationships, but few address the issue of sympathy. It seems that authors often assume that all adults are sympathetic and that nothing more needs to be said.

My years working as a counselor have convinced me that this just isn't true. I find that many people have never learned how to be sympathetic. Others have never learned how to accept sympathy, even when it is given.

Usually, such people don't know that their lives lack sympathy. I find myself having to persuade them that being sympathetic is important. Often, they have no idea how much their lives will change, and how much their relationships will improve, if they learn to give and receive sympathy.

I sometimes use a word picture to illustrate what can happen when sympathy is lacking. Imagine that you're living in prehistoric times. One day while hunting, you accidentally fall and break your arm. Of course, no modern medical techniques exist, so all you can do is live with the pain and hope for the best. If you don't die, it may take a long time for your arm to heal. The outcome is

A house built with the wrong tools will not last; it may not even withstand a mild storm. Trying to build a marriage without the tool of sympathy will not work. Marriages that lack sympathy can't nurture the partners, and the bonds that hold them together soon grow weak. When the storms of life come, the marriage crumbles.

largely a matter of luck. Chances are good that you will be left with an ugly scar and a weakened, perhaps even a crippled, arm.

For many people, it's something like that today when they're hurt emotionally. If those around them haven't learned how to give sympathy, or if the person hasn't learned how to accept it, they simply may be left to heal as best they can. When emotional hurts heal without sympathy, the result is largely a matter of luck. It's like trusting the healing of a broken arm to luck. At best, healing will take a long time. At worst, the hurt never will heal properly. The person may be left emotionally scarred, weakened, even crippled.

When people can't get, or can't accept, the sympathy they need, they often handle their pain in unhealthy ways. We've already talked about alcohol and drug abuse, overeating, workaholism, or having affairs as some destructive ways that people deal with pain when they don't get sympathy.

Transactional Analysis and Your Relationships

Before looking at how sympathy affects marriages and other close relationships, let's discuss a counseling model called *transactional analysis*. This model pictures relationships in a concrete and visual way that many people find helpful.

According to this theory, our personality has three parts: the PARENT, the ADULT, and the CHILD. These have their roots in our actual life experiences. All three exist in every person. They form our character, our personality; they define who we are. The diagram below shows traits that are associated with each part.

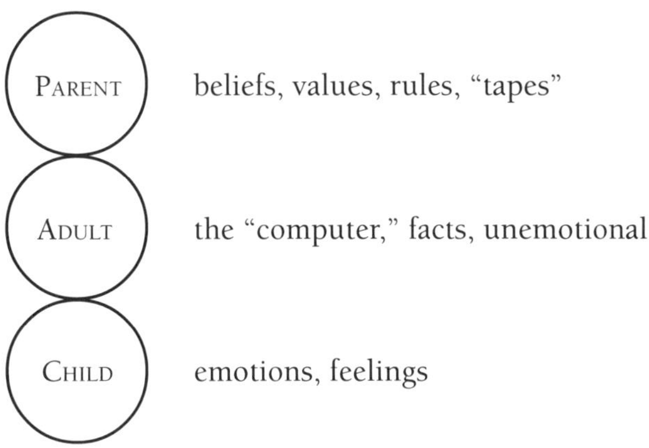

The PARENT part of your personality contains the beliefs, values, and rules by which you live. It also contains "tapes." These are powerful messages learned in childhood. As adults, we tend to play these messages back like tape recordings.

Have you ever found yourself angrily lecturing your child and thought, "I sound just like my dad (or mom)!" If so, you've caught yourself playing a tape.

Usually, we never question the beliefs that underlie tapes. We don't ask ourselves if they are true, nor do we objectively evaluate how useful and important they are in our present circumstances. We accept them without question, and we pass them on without thinking.

For example, if your parents never borrowed money, you may automatically say, "I will never borrow money." If your family opened

Christmas presents on Christmas morning, then you may think that that's the only right time to open Christmas presents. If your parents grew up in poverty or during the Depression, you may feel guilty about not eating every scrap of food on your plate. You may feel this guilt even if you now are rich, have already eaten more than you need or want, and are overweight. Further, you are likely to make your children feel guilty about not eating every bite, too.

These examples show how tapes sometimes can cause problems. Because people feel that their tapes represent "truth," they become angry when others question their taped values. They feel as if the very foundations of their lives are being attacked. It's hard to accept that some cherished "truths" are just learned beliefs. While some of these beliefs may be valuable and useful, some actually may be incorrect or obsolete.

Some counselors say it another way; they say that the PARENT contains "shoulds" learned from our real parents and from other adults. Some "shoulds" are healthy, but some are not.

Now let's talk about the CHILD. The CHILD is the emotional aspect of our personality. It's the CHILD in us that plays, that has feelings and emotions, and enjoys hugs and kisses. It's also the CHILD that enjoys and wants physical or sexual relationships. The CHILD can be the most fun part of our personality.

Unfortunately, just like real children, our inner CHILD may have difficulty being considerate of others. Problems can arise in relationships because of different CHILD needs. For example, the CHILD in you may want to go to the beach while your wife's CHILD prefers going to the mountains. Your CHILD may enjoy staying at home at night and reading a book, while your husband's CHILD may prefer line dancing or bowling.

Just as in a real family, the PARENT and CHILD within us may find themselves in conflict. The ADULT can provide a balance between the rigid rules of the PARENT and the thoughtless needs of the CHILD. The ADULT is the factual, rational, unemotional part of our personality. Some describe it as a computer.

Let's look at an example of how the different parts of the personality can interact and conflict in real relationships. Suppose your husband, in a playful CHILD mode, decides he wants to take you out on the town tonight. Your PARENT tape says, "You can play only when the work's all done." The house is a mess and you still haven't finished the laundry. Your PARENT tape conflicts with your spouse's CHILD needs. If you stay in the PARENT and your spouse stays in the CHILD, an unpleasant argument and slamming doors are a likely result. On the other hand, if you both get into the ADULT, you can discuss your differences and work for a resolution. Perhaps your husband can vacuum while you finish some laundry and then you both can go out on the town and have a great time.

The diagram below shows some of the main interactions possible between the PARENT, the ADULT, and the CHILD of two people—you and your spouse, for example.

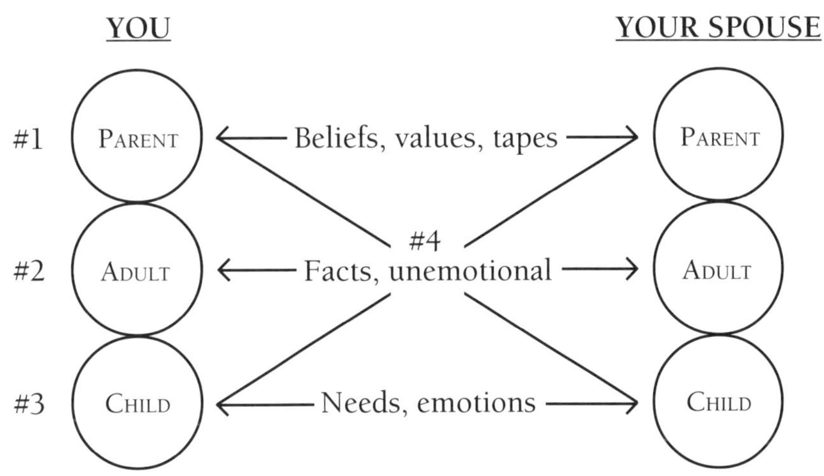

In the diagram, #1 shows the relationship between your PARENT and that of your spouse. How well you get along on a PARENT-to-PARENT level depends in part on how similar, and how different, are your beliefs, values, rules, and tapes.

A second part of your relationship, labeled #2 in the diagram, is the ADULT-to-ADULT level. Both you and your spouse need to have active, healthy ADULTS. It's your ADULT that calmly can discuss differences between the PARENT and the CHILD parts. It takes the objective ADULT to resolve these conflicts and to reach reasonable compromises. Adults are assertive but fair in stating their needs and in listening to the needs of others.

A third part of the relationship, labeled #3, is the CHILD-to-CHILD part. Here, we ask if each partner is comfortable with sharing feelings. Does each like and initiate physical contact, hugs, kisses, and intimacy? Does each like to have fun and, equally important, does each like the same kinds of fun?

Couples can learn a lot about each other, and better understand some of their conflicts, if they explore and discuss their childhood experiences. The environment in which you were raised largely determines the kind of CHILD you have. What was your childhood home like? Were things kept rigidly neat or was the house messy? Did your family eat dinner together? Did you see your parents hug and kiss? Did you see them resolve conflicts calmly or did they fight bitterly? Most important, how did you feel at home? Was home a happy, nurturing place for you as a child, or a place of tension and unpleasantness?

Many adults find that certain events and people in their adult lives trigger the old "at-home" feelings. Your spouse and your children, in particular, may do or say things that bring old feelings flooding back. At such times, many people find themselves either playing back tapes, or acting and feeling as they did in their childhood home. Worse, as they experience these old, at-home feelings and replay tapes, they tend to recreate their childhood home. The unhappy home of childhood can become the unhappy home of adulthood.

My wife and I used to argue about whether our daughter should sleep in our room when she was scared. We probably still would be arguing about it if we hadn't taken the time to discuss each other's childhood.

As a child, my wife sometimes was afraid to go into her bedroom at night. When she would ask her parents to go with her, they simply would say, "You can do it alone; you don't need us."

When our daughter was afraid and wanted to sleep in our bedroom, my wife naturally supported her. She readily identified with Chrissy's feelings.

On the other hand, as a child, I rarely went into my parents' bedroom. It wasn't encouraged. It became my belief that kids shouldn't be allowed in the parents' bedroom. My at-home feeling did not include the presence of children.

Discussing these differences helped us see each other's point of view so that we could resolve our differences. For starters, we agreed that Chrissy could sleep on the floor of our room in a sleeping bag when she was scared. At these times we made a point of talking about her feelings. We listened sympathetically and accepted them without passing judgment on their rightness. As we talked openly about her fears, we had opportunities to help her deal more effectively with them. Finally, we rewarded her for nights that she stayed in her own room. In time, she learned to sleep securely by herself.

Using the transactional analysis model, I describe sympathy as being needed especially in the PARENT-to-CHILD part of the relationship, labeled #4 in the diagram. Are you sympathetic to the CHILD in your spouse, to his or her feelings and needs? Have you ever really thought about his or her feelings and needs?

Most adults readily accept the importance of being sympathetic to young children. If we can take the next step and realize that there is a CHILD hiding inside every adult, it's easier to be receptive to the need for sympathy in our adult relationships. Even strong and capable adults have a fragile and vulnerable CHILD inside them. Let's look at some specific times and circumstances when sympathy is needed most.

When a Person is Sick or Hurt

Certainly sympathy can help a person through an illness or time of depression and frustration. There are many ways to show sympathy to those who are ill or feeling badly. For example, you can make them a meal, do their chores, buy them a magazine, serve their favorite soft drink with a twisty straw, or put an ice pack on their aching head. The possibilities are endless, so I won't even try to list any more. You get the idea.

If you want your sympathy to be most effective, it's best for you to ask your spouse or children what they like when they're feeling ill. In transactional analysis terms, you're being a loving and nurturing PARENT to the CHILD in the other person when you do this.

If you never got much sympathy when you were growing up, you may have trouble letting your spouse give you any now. You may not even tell them when you are feeling sick. When your spouse tries to do nice things for you, you may reject their offers. If they ask how you're feeling, you may say, "I don't want to talk about it."

Some of us grew up with parents who weren't sympathetic or whose tapes said that people should buck up and keep going even when they feel sick. You may have lived with a mother or father who never missed a day of work, no matter how ill they were. Parents who are not sympathetic to their own illnesses are not likely to be sympathetic to those of their children. If you were treated this way, you may have learned your parents' tapes. You may feel that giving sympathy to someone who is ill encourages them to be weak. Actually, it can help a lot if someone simply acknowledges, "Boy, it must be hard having the flu for three weeks."

If you choose to work on being more sympathetic, a good way to start is to ask the hurting person what he or she would like. I remember counseling with a woman who was working on becoming more sympathetic. When her boyfriend was in the hospital for eye surgery, she said to him, "I really care about you, but I'm not sure what you need, so please tell me what I can do." This was great.

It can be particularly hard to deal with someone who thinks you should know automatically what he or she needs and refuses to tell you. It's an irrational belief to think that others are obliged to sense needs. It's best if you can get into your ADULT to talk with the other person about what their hurting CHILD needs. This will require patience and a calm but persistent attitude. Remember, a CHILD can be unreasonable. A hurt CHILD often is scared. Such a CHILD needs a calm, reasonable ADULT to help solve problems.

Helping Someone Who is Facing a Surgery or Medical Test

Sympathy can be very important to those facing medical procedures. Simply saying something like, "I bet you must be a little anxious about the surgery," can be most helpful. Accompanying someone to the hospital or to the doctor's office also can be comforting.

If you aren't used to getting sympathy, you might not even tell others that you're having a test, or you may refuse their offers to go with you. As a young child, I remember seeing my father come home from having his wisdom teeth extracted. He came in the back door, staggered, and then collapsed on the floor. It was frightening to see this large, strong man pass out.

My father had trouble sharing his feelings and allowing others to be sympathetic. My mother knew that he was having teeth pulled that day, but he told her that he didn't want anyone to help him. He drove home by himself, isolated in his pain.

Accepting sympathy helps both the giver and the receiver to feel better. By not accepting our sympathy, my father deprived himself of our comfort, and left the family feeling useless and inadequate.

Helping Someone Deal With a Loss

The death of a parent, a child, or a close friend, for example, is a loss that one needs to grieve. Grieving a loss takes time and requires the support and sympathy of loved ones. The grieving person needs to mourn, to cry, and to express other feelings related to their loss.

In counseling, one woman told me how much she resented that her husband had not gone to either of her parents' funerals. In fact, his score on a temperament test given later suggested that he was quite indifferent to others' feelings.

As a child, he had not been taught how to be sympathetic. He couldn't put himself in his wife's shoes or comfort her in her grief. Unprepared for his response, she was unable to state assertively that she needed his support.

You can give sympathy to a grieving person by holding them, letting them cry in front of you, encouraging them to cry, or by saying something like, "I know you must feel very sad and hurt and angry about your father's death."

When people experience losses, they usually go through some predictable stages of grief shown as a sort of ladder on the diagram below.

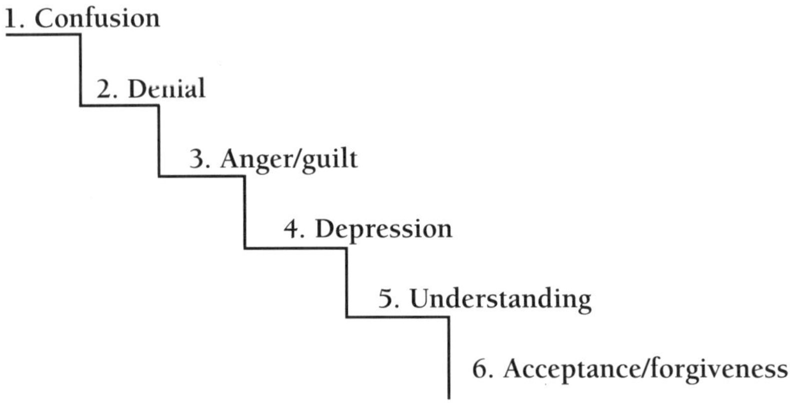

It's important to understand these stages, and to understand that a person can reach acceptance and then fall back again to anger/guilt or depression before reaching a final acceptance.

My wife, Pam, was very sympathetic when my father passed away recently. She allowed, and even encouraged, me to cry. She held me when I cried, and listened whenever I wanted to talk about my dad.

A pastor friend also was helpful. He had dealt previously with his brother's sudden death in a car accident. He said that many people feel waves of grief at such times. In these moments, he encouraged me to let my feelings come to the surface and to express them. The waves did hit me, and I found it helpful just to accept them and to let my feelings flow.

I've learned a lot about grieving since my father died. I now can empathize more easily with others who have lost a loved one.

There's a real danger when such strong feelings don't get expressed through words or tears. Some people try to sink their grief in a flood of alcohol, drugs, or food. The pain can be enormous when a loved one dies. When my father passed away, I remember thinking at first that I didn't want to go on living. When people deal with such intense pain, they desperately need the sympathy of friends and family. The death of a child probably is the biggest loss that a parent ever could experience. It can be especially hard for parents to help one another grieve at such a time, since both are in need of support and neither is able to give it. This is a time for parents to consider counseling. Joining a support group also can be helpful.

By comparison, the death of a pet seems trivial. Many adults have little patience for grief around the death of an animal. Often I have observed situations where a spouse or a parent has been unsympathetic when a family pet dies. It's important to recognize the need to grieve such losses.

A person learns attitudes about losses and grieving as a child. For many children, the first experience of losing a loved one comes with the death of a pet. Children who are told that their sadness is unreasonable or foolish will have a hard time responding appropriately to losses as adults. Also, some children who are forced to bury their feelings at the death of a pet decide that they never again will own one. Such children not only have learned an unhealthy way to deal with pain and grief, they have been cut off unnecessarily from a source of pleasure and comfort.

I remember when our daughter Chrissy's dog, Sugar, died. Chrissy said that she never wanted a pet again. Our son Matt responded sympathetically. He made a large collage of pictures of Sugar and put them in a frame that still hangs in Chrissy's room. I found a special poem about dogs going to Heaven and put it in with the pictures. We all cried about Sugar and we all helped Chrissy deal with her pain. She helped us deal with our pain, too. About six months later, Chrissy surprised us by saying that she'd like another dog for Christmas. Her friends all chipped in to help Chrissy get her new dog. She had grieved Sugar's death and now was able to love a dog again.

I have counseled with many adults who didn't feel that they got support or sympathy when a family pet died. To show sympathy, try saying something like, "I know you must be feeling really sad about your dog's death." It's also a good time to ask your spouse or child what you can do to comfort them.

Helping Someone Deal With the Loss of the "Perfect" Child

If parents are honest with themselves, most will admit that their children have not fulfilled all of their hopes, dreams, and expectations. For example, you may have expected your child to get A's in school but found that B's and C's were the best they could do. Perhaps you felt your child had real musical talent and hoped they would join the school band, but instead they chose to try out for football. Possibly your child has a physical or mental disability. In every case, parents need to grieve the loss of the perfect child and come to accept the child as he or she really is. Only then can parents be more effective in helping children reach their full potential.

The grieving process almost always involves feeling some anger, guilt, and depression. If you can't move beyond these feelings, you won't be effective as a parent. You must reach acceptance of your children in order to help them in healthy ways. Both parents will need to grieve the losses they feel. They can help each other by being sympathetic, offering comfort through hugs or through words. Simply stating the loss, talking about it, and admitting it, is a major first step in moving forward through the grieving process.

Helping Someone When a Child Leaves Home

When a child leaves home to get married, to pursue a career, or to attend college, parents often experience a painful loss. Overcoming this loss can be a complicated process.

I once counseled with a woman to help her grieve the loss when her son enlisted in the Navy. She felt depressed, lost weight excessively, and experienced other physical problems. Her grieving was made difficult because her mother, with whom she lived, was not a sympathetic person. Her son's leaving also triggered old feelings of abandonment. When she was twelve, her mother left her and her sister alone with their father for several months. Now the memory of that painful time came back to her. She was grieving more than just the loss of her son; she was grieving her own childhood abandonment.

The situation became more complicated because she had devoted her life to her son before he left. Her self-worth, her purpose in living, the very scheduling of her days had been focused on the needs of her son. When he was gone, her life became meaningless because there was nothing else in it. Her life was out of balance.

I'm happy to say that this woman now has a job working as a home health aide. She has joined a church and teaches Sunday school; she exercises regularly, and has gone back to school to become a registered nurse. She has created a better, more balanced life for herself. She survived her grief and moved on because she took the initiative to seek counseling. There she found a source of the sympathy and support she needed when none was available to her elsewhere. People need sympathy as they grieve the loss of maturing children.

Helping Someone Deal With the Loss Of a Dream or Goal

Sometimes people need to grieve the loss of a dream or a special goal. Losing an election, being defeated in an athletic event, failing to obtain a publisher for a book, or going unrecognized in a photo or baking contest all are examples of lost dreams and unmet goals. It's surprising how many people are afraid even to admit such defeats for fear that others will think less of them. Simply offering a sincere, "I'm sorry," or "I bet you must be disappointed," can be helpful at such times.

Sympathy Is Needed To Resolve Conflicts

In a marriage it's important for partners to resolve differences that exist between the Parent and Child elements of their personalities. To resolve such conflicts, both need to get together to discuss situations calmly and to work out satisfactory compromises.

The wife can't wait for her husband to get home so that they can go out to dinner, but he's had a bad day at work and is looking forward to a quiet evening at home. It would have helped if the partners had communicated their expectations to each other earlier in the day, but, even then, unexpected events can make it necessary to change plans and expectations. This can be hard for some people to do and it's one place where sympathy is needed in marriages.

I find helpful the following diagram from Norm Wright's book *Marital Counseling* for understanding conflict resolution strategies.

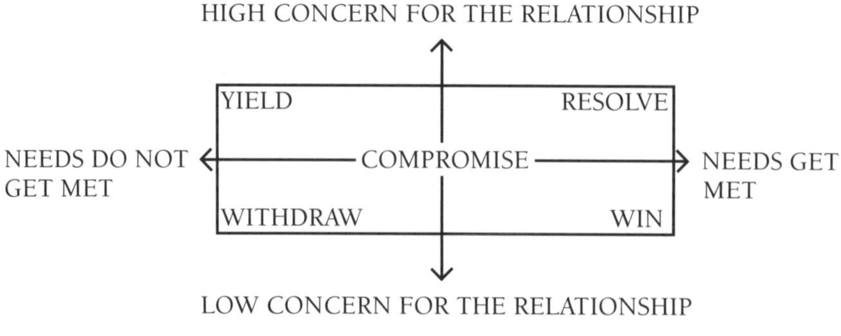

Look at the left side of the diagram. It depicts how those who tend to yield or withdraw in conflicts don't get their needs met. Clearly, that's not good. On the other hand, the right side of the diagram describes those who resolve disagreements or win them. Although these people get their needs met, there's a catch. Just getting needs met isn't enough to maintain a healthy relationship.

You can see one place where problems develop if you look at the bottom of the diagram. Both withdrawing and winning show low concern for the relationship. In fact, withdrawing not only shows low concern, it also means your needs don't get met. This is hardly

Sometimes couples act as if they only know how to debate. Each person may attempt to win, to convince the other that they are right. This shows little sympathy for the needs and ideas of others and gets in the way of solving problems.

the formula for a successful relationship. On the other hand, although winners get their needs met, their long-term relationships suffer because their partners have to lose so that they can win. From this point of view, winners can be losers, too. They get what they want, but destroy their relationships in the process of winning.

The top of the diagram illustrates another potential problem area. Although yielding shows high concern for the relationship, you pay for this concern at the expense of not getting your needs met. If you always yield in the face of a conflict, then your resentments are sure to grow. Your relationships can't succeed.

The healthiest option is to resolve conflicts by seeking a win-win solution. When this happens, the needs of both partners get met. The relationship prospers because the partners consider not only their own needs but those of each other as well. Although it may not be possible to meet each partner's needs with absolute equality on every issue, still, there is a feeling that everyone wins when people resolve problems. This same feeling isn't there if you withdraw or yield. Even compromising may be less satisfactory.

Let's be sure this last point is clear. Suppose you want to go to bed at 9:00 and your spouse wants to go to bed at 10:00. You could compromise on 9:30 but that really doesn't meet either person's needs. This is especially true if the reason your spouse wants to stay up is to watch a favorite TV program that's on till 10:00. You could resolve this conflict by staying up till 10:00 on the night of your spouse's TV show and going to bed at 9:00 on the following night.

To resolve conflicts, each person must be in the ADULT mode. This means talking calmly and rationally, and listening sympathetically. The partners must care about each other's needs and be willing to consider both points of view. People who only act to win conflicts are probably in the dominating PARENT mode. They insist that their viewpoints are the right ones. They think their personal beliefs and values represent facts or truth. When people take this unsympathetic attitude, it's almost impossible for them to resolve conflicts. They simply can't allow themselves to listen to or acknowledge other points of view. They have set themselves up as defenders of right against wrong. Compromise and resolution are not possible.

A similar problem can arise when a person is in the CHILD mode. Children can be stubborn or selfish, insisting on having things their way. Usually, though, children tend to yield or withdraw. They may feel fearful to speak up, lacking the self-esteem to express their views, especially when they contradict those of a PARENT. In either case, conflicts are unlikely to be resolved.

A key to conflict resolution is the ability of each person to be sympathetic, to care about the other person's feelings, opinions, and needs. Without this tool, it's impossible for a couple to reach a win-win solution. If you only care about your needs, then having things your way is all that counts.

Husbands and wives have difficulty resolving conflicts when the partners have no sympathy for each other's needs and viewpoints. Couples may spend more time blaming one another for conflicts than they do looking for sympathetic ways to resolve them.

Sympathy Is Needed When Decisions Are Made

It's easy for couples to get into difficulties when important decisions must be made. Often the partners have different expectations about who should be involved in decision-making. Couples need to talk about who will have input.

For example, a husband may feel that all car buying decisions should be his because he knows more about cars. His wife, on the other hand, may feel that she has a right to some input. After all, she has to live with the car, too, and wants specific features that she likes.

Partners need to be sympathetic to each other's needs and to resolve conflicts in sharing decision-making power. Partners also need to realize that they will reach decisions at different rates. One partner may look at cars for two days and feel satisfied with a particular car, while his spouse may need two weeks. It's important to be sympathetic and allow your mate to have the time he or she needs before expecting discussion or agreement.

Sympathy Is Needed When Showing Love to Your Spouse

In English there is only one word for love. In Greek, there are three. *Eros* is the sexual or sensual aspect of love. *Philia* is the friendship aspect of love. Though both are important, marriages can't last without the third aspect, *agape*.

Agape is the decision to love. It's giving love purposefully, not just because you feel like it at the moment, but instead as an active decision, perhaps in the face of contrary feelings.

For example, choosing to iron a shirt for your spouse when you're tired could be an example of *agape* love. Taking your wife square dancing, even though you don't like to dance, is an example of *agape* love, especially if you go with a purposefully happy heart instead of a grouchy, complaining mood.

A common problem for many couples is that they don't tell each other what their language of love is. If so, you may show love to your spouse in ways that you would like, but not in ways that he or she can appreciate.

For example, maybe you like receiving flowers, so you send flowers to your spouse. He doesn't respond. Now you feel disappointed and hurt. The problem may be that flowers aren't his language of love. He might prefer a set of baseball cards. Though your intent in sending the flowers was loving and sympathetic, your spouse would experience that love and sympathy more if you had given him cards. Both of you need to tell each other about your language of love.

A helpful exercise is for each partner to write down his or her language of love and share it with his or her spouse. I recommend stating at least three things you would like in each area of love: *eros, philia, and agape*. This way, partners have a menu of what their mate needs to feel loved.

This man hasn't been sympathetic to his wife's needs or to her "language of love." His mixing bowl gift reflects what he thinks she "should" need, not what she wants. He may feel that she is being ungrateful when she shows her disappointment, but he is as much at fault as she is.

Notice that *agape* love can be applied to *eros* or *philia* love situations. For example, you might decide to make love because your spouse wants to, even though you feel no particular desire or need for sex at that time. This is *agape* love in an *eros* love situation. Or you might decide to go for a walk with your spouse because they want to be with you for a quiet moment together. It's a nice idea, but you're tired and your feet hurt. Still, you choose to go. This is *agape* love in a *philia* love situation.

Sympathy is important when couples want to show concern and communicate love. If your spouse truly is to feel your love, you must think of their needs from their viewpoint. You must learn to speak their language of love. This is the essence of *agape*, of sympathy, the lost aspect of love.

Helping Someone Deal With Midlife Crisis Issues

I believe it's a mistake to treat the midlife crisis as some sort of joke. Parties with black balloons, black cups, and cards of sympathy may have a place as a rite of passage, but the midlife crisis also can be a genuinely difficult moment for many people. Because we tend to trivialize midlife crisis issues, people have difficulty recognizing and accepting that this time is a natural and normal moment of life transition.

Just as a young child begins to walk at ten months, talk at twelve months, and speak in sentences at thirty months, so, too, do adults begin to question their lives between the ages of thirty and fifty. It's about this time that many people begin to experience the loss of physical appearance, of physical stamina, and of sexual drive. It may become more difficult to recover from illnesses and injuries, and they may become more frequent, as well. Children leave home for college, marriage, and careers.

In midlife, people also must let go of unrealistic dreams about career and material goals. Not everything we hoped for in our youth comes to pass. This is a loss that can hurt. Many begin to question what they have done with their lives and to wonder what they will do with what remains. When one's parents die, the inevitable reality of one's own death also becomes more apparent. Women who have based their identity on motherhood may have special difficulty as they find themselves no longer needed by their children. These are the serious issues that people face as they reach the midlife years. Such issues are the reason that midlife truly can be experienced as a crisis.

The difficulties of midlife can be handled more effectively when people are reassured that their doubts and problems are normal. They need plenty of sincere sympathy. Sympathetic statements like, "I bet it's tough now that the kids have left home," or "It must be hard to accept that you didn't get that promotion," really help a struggling person who needs to know that others see the pain they face. Don't forget, the best way to find out what kind of sympathy someone needs is to ask them.

Sympathy Is Needed When You Apologize to Someone

What do you do if you've hurt someone? Do you apologize or do you simply withdraw? Sympathy is needed to apologize to someone you've hurt.

It's impossible for a couple always to be in harmony. Conflicts will occur, disappointments will come up, expectations will go unmet, and needs will be ignored at times. In all these situations, simply saying, "I'm sorry," can help restore harmony.

It's definitely wrong to think, "Love is never having to say you're sorry." If you're sympathetic and concerned about your partner's feelings, you'll be more able, and more willing, to apologize for your mistakes. In fact, sympathetic love is what makes it possible to mean it when you say, "I'm sorry."

Forgiving Those Who Have Hurt You

I sometimes use a word picture to describe the grudges and resentments that people may hold. I say that such resentments are like handcuffs binding you to those you resent.

Imagine yourself chained to someone who hurt you in the past. It would be unpleasant to be forced to endure constant contact with such a person. Worse, if you went around handcuffed to someone from your past, it would be hard to meet or get close to anyone new.

Forgiving those who have hurt you releases the handcuffs and lets you form healthy relationships now and in the future.

There are many books that discuss forgiveness. Some of my favorites are *Making Peace with Your Parents* by Harold Bloomfield, *Making Peace with Your Past* by Norm Wright, and *Making Peace with Your Father* by Dr. David Stoop. It has always seemed to me that forgiving often requires a missing ingredient—sympathy. Few books address the importance of sympathy to the process of forgiving.

If a parent, a sibling, a close family friend, or some other adult hurt you, you may continue to harbor resentments toward them. Perhaps your parents never spent time with you, or were domineering, or alcoholic. In many ways, everyone has been hurt as a child. You have every right to be angry with those who hurt you, and you probably are. It's this anger, though, that binds you to your painful past. To break free, to move on and leave your pain behind, forgiveness is necessary. It's especially hard to forgive those who hurt you badly.

An important step is understanding the other person's past. For example, if you found out that your mother also grew up with a domineering mother, or that her parents also were alcoholics, this insight could help you understand why she behaved toward you as she did. However, just knowing the past often is not enough.

It's easy to get stuck thinking, *So what? She still should have done something different. She was a grown-up; I was just a child.* It's easy, but it's a mistake. Remember, forgiving—letting go of resentments—is for your benefit, not for the benefit of those who hurt you. You're the one that still suffers the hot pain of old resentments. You're the one whose life doesn't move on. You're the one who's handcuffed to the past.

This is where you need the healing power of sympathy. It's the ability to see life from the other person's viewpoint that makes it possible to let go of resentments. Without sympathy, it can be difficult or impossible to forgive.

I've counseled with many adults who harbored old resentments. For most, an important part of attaining the freedom of forgiveness was understanding the importance of sympathy, and then learning how to be more sympathetic.

I once counseled with a man who said he didn't have time to forgive his father. As we talked, I realized that a real barrier was this man's view of his father as some sort of a gigantic monster with horns. I worked to help him see his father instead as a six-year-old child who never had a chance to grow up healthy. I knew that if he could do this, he could begin to consider more forgiving and sympathetic thoughts.

Eventually, this man remembered hearing how his father had to go to work when he was very young. He began to realize that his father's childhood didn't include playing and having fun. No one ever had had time for him. As he came to accept this point of view, he also could accept why his father had trouble giving him the attention that he had craved. This new perspective freed him to think sympathetically of his father's struggles and pains. When he could do this, the handcuffs that had bound him to the gigantic monster with horns fell away, and he was on the road to freedom.

Undoubtedly, during the past day, week, or month you've been hurt by some action of your spouse, of a friend, or of your child. Perhaps they yelled at you, were critical, or forgot your birthday. Each and every day, we need to forgive those around us for their hurtful actions, both intentional and unintentional. If you're sympathetic, you'll be more able to put yourself in another's place. You'll understand why they acted as they did. You'll be able to forgive. When you forgive, you avoid building walls of hardened grudges that can forever separate you from others.

Don't forget that the more you know about your spouse's childhood, the more you'll be able to understand their present behavior and actions. That knowledge, combined with your own active sympathy, will help you accept and forgive them. Truly, forgiving others is the key to your freedom.

Points to Ponder:

1. Identify areas where you need or have needed more sympathy in your life. Share your thoughts about this with your spouse.
2. Discuss some specific ways that you would like your spouse to show sympathy.
3. Is there someone in your past that you need to forgive? If so, make a commitment to start the forgiving process now. Remember that you are freeing yourself by forgiving them.

Chapter 6

What Should I Do If My Spouse Is Not Sympathetic?

In spite of "seeing" sympathy in their families, children may not act as sympathetic adults if no one specifically teaches them how to be sympathetic. You may have to be assertive with such adults, telling them exactly what you need, even though you think your needs should be obvious.

Experience has taught me that the way a person thinks about a problem can make it better or worse. Even easily manageable problems can appear impossibly large and intimidating if they are distorted through a filter of unreasonable beliefs and expectations. On the other hand, if we adjust our beliefs and expectations, if we make them more rational, our problems become more manageable. The diagram below illustrates this viewpoint.

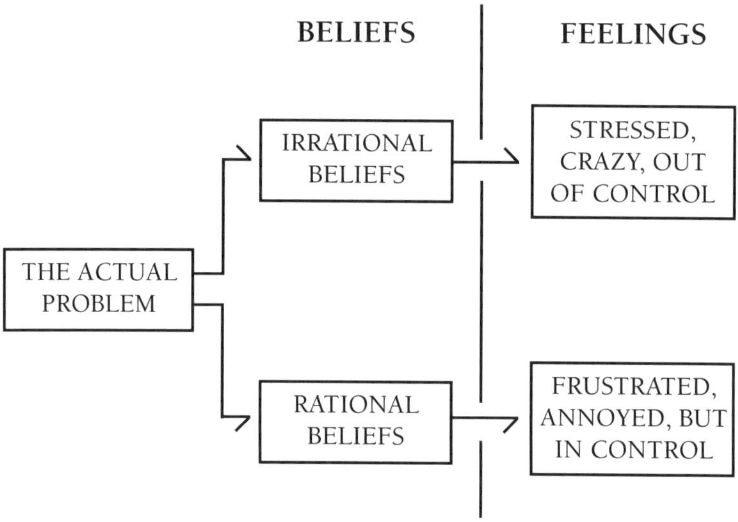

For example, let's assume that your spouse treats you unsympathetically. If you filter this actual problem through a belief that he or she "should" be sympathetic, its lack will cause you to feel stressed and crazy. Believing that others "should" act in some specific way is irrational. Thinking that something "should" happen only sets us up to be stressed if it doesn't. When we feel stressed, we're more likely either to attack others or to withdraw. Both responses are unproductive, even harmful. Worse, if you believe that others can make you feel badly, you've given them the power to determine how you feel. You will feel powerless and out of control. After all, they're controlling you; you aren't controlling yourself. Feeling stressed, powerless, crazy, and out of control won't help you handle your spouse's lack of sympathy. In fact, if nothing changes, it's likely that things will grow worse. So what's your alternative?

First, you need to examine how your beliefs are contributing to how you feel. Remember, it's not so much what others do that causes your feelings; it's the way you view what they do. In this sense, your beliefs determine your feelings.

You have control over what you believe. This means you also have some control over how you feel, even though you can't control what happens to you.

The key is looking at your spouse's lack of sympathy in another way. If you work to change your view, to make it more rational, you'll be more able to state your needs in ways your spouse can accept.

For example, a more rational belief would be to tell yourself that your spouse might never have learned how to be sympathetic. Perhaps they rarely saw sympathy modeled in their childhood home. If you look at the problem in this way, it's easier to remain calm and objective.

You're not a robot, so you still may feel frustrated and annoyed, but you can reduce the amount of stress you feel, and you don't have to go crazy. You are in control of yourself. Remaining calm in response to your spouse's lack of sympathy is the first step.

The next step is choosing the appropriate moment and way to approach your spouse. If you catch them off guard with your request for sympathy, or at a time when they're feeling low or upset, he's likely to resist any changes you suggest. They simply may refuse to do what you ask, or may attack you for your faults and shortcomings.

The most effective way to express your views is to be assertive. Remain firm in your position and keep restating your needs in a calm and steady voice. This is the heart of assertive behavior. You may find it helps to say something like, "I don't think that you were being sympathetic about my needs when you . . . " Before saying this sort of thing, it's usually good to ask the other person if they're open to hearing about your feelings. You want to find out if they are able to be receptive. If they aren't, it may be better to wait for a more appropriate time. When you're assertive, you're acting out of love—love and respect for yourself and for the other person.

Being assertive in stating your needs may not be enough. You also will have to learn how to be persistent when your spouse makes a countermove. Harriet Lerner's book, *The Dance of Anger*, discusses effective and ineffective ways to handle anger and typical countermoves. Ms. Lerner says something that I find valuable.

> Our job is to keep clear about our own position in the face of a countermove; not to prevent it from happening or to tell the other person that he or she should not be reacting that way. Most of us want the impossible. We want to control not only our own decisions and choices but also the other person's reactions to them. We not only want to make a change; we want the other person to like the change that we make. We want to move ahead to a higher level of assertiveness and clarity and then receive praise and reinforcement from those very people who have chosen us for our old familiar ways.

In other words, you need to realize and accept that others will make countermoves. Don't get upset by these, just accept them as normal. You must keep reminding yourself that it takes time and persistence to get the sympathy you need. It helps if you can be very specific about what your needs are. You can't assume that others automatically know them. Surprisingly, this can be a special problem for those who are themselves sympathetic by nature or training. Such people often assume others know what they want and need without having to be told. Remember, it's a little like learning to speak a new language. A lot of help and practice is necessary. Those around you will require occasional reminders of what you need when they aren't being sympathetic.

If it's hard for you to discuss such issues with your spouse, try putting your thoughts, feelings, and suggestions in writing. Sometimes people are more receptive to the written word.

When you write, start by praising your spouse for the things he or she does that you appreciate most. Then, be factual about stating where you feel sympathy has been lacking. Tell them specifically what you'd like in the future. Suggest a time to get together to discuss what you've written. Even better, ask your spouse

Many adults refuse to accept help from others even when it's quite apparent that they need it. As children, such people may have learned not to count on others and to try to handle all their problems by themselves.

to respond in writing. This lets both partners state their views assertively and gives each some time to consider what the other has said before responding. If you give the letter to your spouse on their way to work, they will have time to think about what you're saying.

Before writing this letter to your spouse, you may need to write a kind of practice letter first, one that you won't actually send to them. Over the years resentments may have built up because of the lack of sympathy in your relationship. You may need to work through these resentments first, express them, and let them out in your practice letter before you can write a truly constructive letter.

I encouraged one woman who had been married for over twenty-five years to write such a letter. She listed over thirty specific situations where her husband had not been sympathetic. On her list were items such as never helping with the babies, never helping with discipline, never asking how his wife's day had gone, never accepting any of her ideas, and constantly putting her down. The list went on and on. Sometimes such a letter is simply too volatile, too explosive to share with a spouse point-blank. Some kinds of strong resentments built up over many years may need to be shared and discussed with a counselor first.

This example says a lot about the two people involved. The husband had never been taught how to be sympathetic. Perhaps he had never observed a man being sympathetic to a woman in his childhood family. The wife grew up in a dysfunctional family herself where she was not allowed or encouraged to express her pain. She learned as a child to pretend when she was hurting. She continued to use this strategy as an adult in her marriage. She pretended when she was in pain until she could no longer stand to pretend. Then, with years of built-up resentments, she moved out of her marriage altogether. Currently, she and her husband are attempting to reconcile. Her husband was willing to read her "angry" letter. This was a sympathetic act that has helped his wife heal her past hurts. Reading the letter also has given him some very specific understandings about what his wife needs in the way of sympathy.

It's important for couples to discuss and learn about each other's childhood experiences. Working together, partners can see how they may not have learned to be sympathetic or how to accept sympathy in their childhood homes. This process develops more rational beliefs and expectations and can help you be more sympathetic to each other's needs. A good way to begin is for both partners to complete the "Survey on Sympathy" in chapter 3 of this book. Discuss your answers with each other.

Don't be discouraged if you find that changing is difficult. It's hard to learn any new skill. There also are some subtle reasons that can make learning sympathy especially difficult. For example, many people marry someone who's like one of their parents. Sometimes people make such choices consciously; sometimes they're not aware of their motives. If your parents weren't sympathetic, it's quite possible that you may have sought out an unsympathetic partner. Naturally, such a spouse won't respond quickly to your requests for more sympathy. He or she may be argumentative about your needs or may simply dismiss you as ridiculous.

In the next chapter, we'll talk more about things that make it hard to become sympathetic. We'll also discuss some obstacles that you'll have to overcome in getting your mate to be more sympathetic. You'll need to deal with these as you explore the issue of sympathy and changing your relationship.

Chapter 7
Why Is It Hard to Become More Sympathetic?

In this chapter we'll talk about things that make it hard to become more sympathetic. We'll also look at why it can be hard to help your spouse become more sympathetic. When you've identified the issues blocking your way, you can begin working to remove them. We'll also suggest some extra readings if you want to learn more about particular areas. Remember that a professional counselor can help you make the most rapid and most complete progress.

When In Pain, Pretend

As children, many adults were not allowed to express painful feelings. Often their parents believed that it was better to ignore unpleasant feelings than to discuss them openly.

During counseling, a woman once told me how her two-year-old brother drowned in the backyard swimming pool when she was fourteen. The family never talked about it. One Christmas, as her grandmother showed some old family slides, several pictures of her brother came up. Her mother told the grandmother to remove those pictures and never show them again.

This woman experienced tremendous pain when her infant brother died, but her parents didn't encourage, or even allow, her to talk about it. They prevented her from grieving her loss and forced her to pretend that everything was fine, rather than helping her deal with her feelings. Because she did not acknowledge the pain, it did not go away. It pursued her into her adult life, affecting her marriage and her other relationships.

When painful things happen to adults who have repressed childhood feelings, they may handle the pain by returning to the strategies of their childhood. They pretend. They don't talk about how they feel. They ignore the pain and act as though nothing has happened. Above all, they try to tell themselves that they're not really hurting.

Children often feel powerless when painful things happen. Unless they are taught healthy ways to handle feelings, this sense

Many adults make it hard for others to be sympathetic. They may not express their needs, or they may deny that they're hurting, even when their pain is obvious to others.

of inadequacy in the face of pain can be carried over into their adult relationships. They may feel that there's nothing they can do to make things better. Often, they are right. If you are powerless, if you pretend that pain isn't there, you're trapped. After all, you can't fix something that doesn't exist. You first must admit that the pain is there before you can begin to fix it.

In counseling, an important first goal is to stop pretending about pain. People must realize that they're no longer helpless children. They must learn to see themselves as adults with the power to improve their lives.

Ignorance About What's Required to Improve a Relationship

Recently, a man in counseling told me that his marriage had been unsatisfactory for some time. His wife had shared this same feeling in an earlier session. The couple had three teenagers. The man said he thought that things would get better after the kids left home. His hope was that his marriage would somehow improve without either him or his wife having to make any changes. I used a word picture to help him see how unreasonable this attitude was.

I suggested that he imagine himself driving in a car with three teenagers. The engine is not running well. It constantly misses and backfires. The car is barely chugging along. After a while, the three teenagers get out and walk off on their own. Will the engine now run better?

Such an idea is absurd! Everyone knows that some positive action is needed if the engine is to run more smoothly. Someone will have to get the right tools and then do some work to fix whatever's wrong.

We see this easily enough when we're talking about cars. Why don't we see it when it's our marriages and relationships that aren't working well? The principle is exactly the same. If a marriage is barely chugging along, one, or usually both, partners will need to get some new tools and learn how to use them if the marriage is to run better.

When we're in pain, we lapse far too often into pretending, feeling powerless, or simply expecting the other person to do the changing.

It's easy to point to what someone else could do to improve a relationship. It's a lot harder to take responsibility for adding tools to our own marriage tool kits and then learning how to use them.

Blaming Others for Problems or Blaming Ourselves Excessively

The term *codependent* sometimes is used to describe people who grew up in dysfunctional families. Such families unintentionally teach harmful ways to handle situations and people. One typical codependent trait is blaming others for problems. I once saw a cartoon that illustrated this perfectly. A husband and wife are visiting a marriage counselor. The wife leans across the desk, points to her husband and says, "Our problem is him."

At least this couple was doing one thing right. They sought counseling. Unfortunately, many codependents never do, because they expect someone else to do all the changing. Codependent men tend to point to people and things outside themselves as the cause of problems. They distance themselves from responsibility for problems and from any need to change their behavior.

Codependent women, on the other hand, often are too hard on themselves when things go wrong. They may become immobilized with guilt to the point that they are unable to make necessary changes.

Some Adults Make it Hard for Others To Be Sympathetic

Many adults never talk much about their feelings. They make it difficult for their spouse or anyone else to give them sympathy. If others don't know when you're in pain, can't tell when you're disappointed, or discouraged, or are greeted with sarcasm when they ask how you're feeling, how can they be expected to act sympathetically?

I once counseled with a doctor who was working on becoming more sympathetic. He told about an occasion when he noticed that his wife's eye looked sore and irritated. Trying to show sympathy, he offered to examine it. Unfortunately, she also had a tendency to be unsympathetic. Like many people who lack sympathy, she had difficulty accepting it from others. Angrily she responded,

"No! I don't need you to check it." The next morning it was much worse. Only then did she accept help from her husband.

This man's first attempt to show sympathy was rejected. Unfortunately, he was new at the art of being sympathetic, so he couldn't get beyond his wife's initial resistance. Giving sympathy to others is not always easy. It requires persistence.

The Belief That Discussing Painful Feelings Is Not Helpful

I once explained the need for sympathy to a man whose marriage was falling apart. As we discussed the importance of talking about feelings, he happened to mention that his oldest daughter had just left home for college. I asked how he and his wife felt about this. He said that his wife seemed upset and depressed, but that he hadn't actually discussed the loss with her.

His own reaction was, "All kids grow up and leave home. What's there to talk about? I mean, if the dog dies, well, everyone knows that dogs die; all dogs die. So why talk about it?" Here was a man who was no help to his partner as she grieved losing the child who had moved away. As I tried to explain the importance of listening to his wife's feelings, this man became argumentative. I asked him how he handled his feelings.

He said, "All my life I've just held them in. If things get too unpleasant or difficult, I go out and play golf to get away for a while. Why should I change now? My way has worked all my life."

Sometimes questions like this stump me, but this time the answer seemed clear. I asked if his way of handling feelings was helping his marriage. He had to admit that it wasn't.

This man believed that pain was something to be ignored or suffered in silence. As we talked, he realized that he had learned this belief in childhood. It now prevented him from becoming more sympathetic. He needed to change his way of thinking if his marriage was to improve. Most adults don't know that they've developed destructive belief systems about life. They feel that the ways they handle life situations are the same ways everyone uses. They don't realize that better alternatives exist, and that it's within their power to learn them.

Being Defensive Makes it Hard to Become More Sympathetic

People who take suggestions defensively have trouble becoming more sympathetic. Let's face it; it's hard to change if you put all your energy into proving that nothing needs changing. The transactional analysis model can be helpful here so let's look at it again.

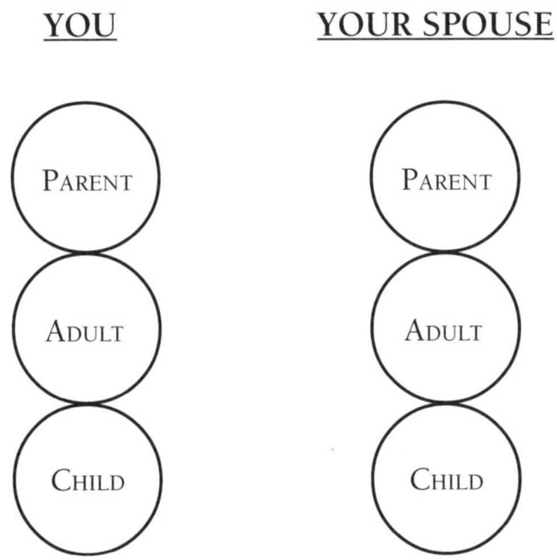

Unfortunately, some people take suggestions or requests in their Child. They become defensive. They may view the person making suggestions as a scolding Parent telling them that they're wrong or bad, or as a nagging, demanding Parent trying to force them to do something they don't want to do, or as a controlling Parent trying to manipulate and maneuver them against their will. How can you get your needs met and avoid such unproductive relationships?

Let's suppose that your Child needs something that it's not getting, maybe a hug or some comforting words. If you communicate your needs while in the Child mode, your partner probably will hear and respond to you either from their Parent ("Oh, grow up and stop whining!") or from their Child ("You think you have it bad; well, I've got it worse"). He or she may dig in their heels and resist, or may retaliate by pointing out your faults and reminding you of your shortcomings. In any case, they will have a hard time being sympathetic to your needs.

People with low self-esteem can quickly become defensive when questioned or confronted about their behavior. It's important to be sympathetic at such times, although it can be hard to do. Often it's best to defer discussing an issue. It can be helpful to write a short note to the other person describing your feelings and needs. This gives them time to consider their response and reduces their immediate impulse to become defensive.

Your CHILD needs are most likely to be met if you first get into your ADULT. Don't whine or demand like a child; state your needs reasonably and calmly like an adult. Now your partner can hear your needs in their ADULT. Being in the ADULT helps him or her consider your request logically and makes your partner more able to meet your needs reasonably. It gives your spouse the chance to act sympathetically.

Being defensive has other causes, too. Some people grow up with nagging, coercive parents who constantly boss them around. As children, they unconsciously may vow that, "When I grow up, no one will tell me what to do." They may continue to follow this child vow even as adults, though they probably won't be aware of it. They show it's there by the way they act. For example, people who put things off to annoy or frustrate others, especially others they see as bossy, demanding parents, are displaying a sign that this vow still is operating.

Adults who maintain child vows not to let others "tell them what to do" find themselves in constant conflict. As an example, imagine a wife who asks her husband to call her if he's going to be late from work. He takes this request in his CHILD and mutters to himself, "Why should I call her? She's not my mother." He resents the need to check in with a person he sees as a controlling PARENT. What might he do differently?

He would feel less resentment, and less stress, if he took the request in his PARENT. Making the call to his wife then would be an act of parental reassurance so that her CHILD wouldn't worry if he was late.

He would do even better if he took an ADULT perspective. Then he would see his wife's request as a reasonable, ADULT need; after all, she has to plan dinner. This viewpoint produces the least stress and makes it easier to act sympathetically.

Notice that when the husband takes his wife's request defensively, he can act neither as a positive parent to his wife's CHILD, nor as a cooperative adult partner. He's just a demanding, needy child. This is a recipe for problems in a marriage.

Another communication problem sometimes occurs when one partner tries to tell the other what makes him or her feel sexually fulfilled. If this is taken as criticism, both partners may slip into the CHILD. What started as two adults talking about what they need to feel pleasure may become two whining children arguing on the playground.

Discussing sexual needs is a normal and necessary part of communication in marriage. Partners learn to know and respect each other's likes and dislikes by staying in the ADULT and avoiding defensiveness. Remember, adults can consider requests rationally and can act reasonably to meet needs. Children can't.

You can recognize if your partner takes your requests in the CHILD by his or her reaction. They may get angry and complain about some related, or unrelated, thing that you have done incorrectly. They may withdraw and stop communicating at all. In such cases, they are unlikely to comply with your requests or suggestions.

When this happens, it's important for you to remain in the Adult. Talk calmly about your feelings and needs. You must make it clear that you simply are stating your needs, not being critical. Be a "broken record." Calmly repeat the same idea. Doing this gives your partner a chance to get into their Adult and to consider what you've said unemotionally.

If your spouse remains defensive, try putting your feelings in writing. Later, when the Child feelings have had a chance to cool, share your letter. I talk about this technique in chapter 6, entitled "What Should I Do If My Spouse Is Not Sympathetic?"

The important thing is to avoid giving up. Be reasonable but persistent in discussing issues with your spouse. Since many adults felt powerless to change things when they were children, they bring feelings of powerlessness into their marriages. Remind yourself that you aren't a child anymore; you aren't powerless. You're an adult who can make things happen. You can bring about change.

The Tendency To Be Too Objective

"Don't cry over spilt milk." Some adults heard this constantly as they grew up. I once counseled with a woman who discovered how little sympathy she had for others when her husband became seriously ill. One day, after a series of lab tests, they lingered in a doctor's waiting room. Her husband sat tensely, dreading to hear the diagnosis.

His wife could have consoled him with a sympathetic comment like, "I bet you're worried about those tests. It's frightening when you don't know what's wrong." Instead, she added to her husband's misery by dwelling on the money problems they had now that he was no longer able to work.

Looking back on this, she realized that her lack of sympathy started in childhood. She grew up on a farm where her parents taught her to accept disappointments stoically. Bad years and failed crops are a part of farming. When confronted by disappointments, her farmer parents simply set out to find practical solutions.

The problem was that her parents treated everything in the same stoical way. They never acknowledged, or even discussed, their daughter's childish fears about what might happen to the family when crops failed.

Many adults grew up in a family where the attitude was "Here's a quarter, call someone who cares." When one grows up in this environment they soon learn to repress their feelings since there will be no sympathy

Later in life, when she lost a boyfriend, she got no sympathy for her tears. "There are always other men," her practical parents reminded her.

This woman came to think that all life's problems could be managed and controlled if only she remained sufficiently objective. To be a good farmer it's necessary to be objective. Unfortunately, this woman's parents used the same approach for raising children that they used for raising corn. Being a good parent requires some different skills from those needed to be a good farmer. Sometimes people need sympathy more than they need solutions.

I Shouldn't Have To Tell Others My Needs; They Should Know Them

Some people believe that grownups shouldn't have to tell others what they need. This belief short-circuits the process of expressing needs and receiving sympathy.

No one knows what you need better than you do. Unfortunately, no one can read your mind. If you want your spouse to do something different, you first have to tell them what you need.

It's irrational to expect others magically to know what your needs are. Nothing could be more unreasonable than believing, "If my spouse truly loved me, they would know what I need." It's unfair to expect people to meet you more than halfway. In a genuinely loving relationship, both partners must carry their share. If you want your needs to be met, it's your responsibility to express them clearly and openly. Love has many powers, but it's foolish to expect it to make your spouse telepathic.

The Tendency To Recreate Your "At-Home" Feeling

There is a tendency in marriages for each partner to recreate their "at-home" feeling. If you came from a happy, loving childhood home, this feeling can be positive. If your home was an angry, sad, or critical place, this "at-home" feeling may be negative.

For example, if you rarely received sympathy in your childhood home, then your adult "at-home" feeling may involve structuring your life and relationships to avoid getting sympathy. When others offer sympathy, you may reject it. You may say you don't want to talk about painful issues, or you simply may resist telling people anything about how you're feeling. No matter what your technique is, you'll tend to act in ways that recreate the old "at-home" feeling of never getting sympathy.

When people recreate an unhealthy "at-home" feeling, they tend to do it subconsciously. That can make it difficult to change. People don't realize what they're doing. It's impossible to fix a problem if you don't even know it exists.

A common source of negative "at-home" feelings is neglect. As children, most people experience some degree of neglect. In America our material needs for food, clothing, and shelter usually are met. It's our emotional needs that may not have been satisfied.

Your parents need not have abandoned you on the neighbors' doorstep for you to feel emotionally neglected. They need not have beaten you, or locked you in a closet. Feelings of neglect can come from much more ordinary experiences.

Perhaps your parents rarely praised you, advised you, or helped you set goals. Such mundane experiences may cause feelings of neglect that can have important effects on your adult life.

Neglect often is hard for adults to identify because it comes from an absence of something rather than its presence. How do you know that something's missing if you never experienced having it?

Although neglect can be as emotionally damaging as physical abuse, adults are much less likely to seek help for related problems. If you were physically abused as a child, you don't usually forget the incidents and how painful they were. If you later have problems in life connected with the abuse, you know you need help, and you know where to begin looking for answers.

The effects of neglect are harder to identify, because the neglect itself may have been quite subtle. It also may be harder to accept that neglect is the source of problems, because its relationship to your adult behavior and experiences may not be obvious.

As an adult, there are many ways you may respond to the neglect you experienced as a child. For example, you may hold your feelings in and never share them with your spouse, or you may resist accepting sympathy from your partner. Perhaps you create distance by constantly finding fault or by arguing and picking fights.

If you are using such strategies to create distance in your marriage, you may want to read more about the subject of emotional neglect. An excellent book that discusses this issue and other destructive parenting styles is W. Hugh Missildine's *Your Inner Child of the Past*.

Did Your Parents Overindulge You?

Overindulging children is one way to make it hard for them ever to become sympathetic adults. Children whose parents overindulge them often continue to think only of themselves when they become adults. They have little experience or skill in thinking of others. The following paragraph, taken from Missildine's *Your Inner Child of the Past*, sums this up:

> When the overindulged child grows up, he has difficulty in coping with the demands of reality. He tends to blame others for his being deprived of the cornucopia of childhood. Because of the close relationships existing in his childhood, he tends to be attractive and charming, moving quickly and easily into close relationships. But he expects as his automatic right the unlimited goods and services he had in childhood. When the relationship requires that he contribute, he cannot comply easily and often turns against the partner in his disappointment. Often the indulged person hurts those closest to him.

If you or your spouse were overindulged as children, you need to consider this. You may have to work on changing your tendency to expect others to meet your needs without you being obliged to consider theirs.

What If You Get No Support for Changing or Asking for Sympathy?

Sometimes when a person starts acting more sympathetically, their spouse may not encourage the change. After all, the partners may have chosen each other originally to recreate at-home feelings of not getting sympathy. Changing may make your partner feel uncomfortable or threatened.

Unfortunately, if a new behavior gets no support or encouragement, it's unlikely to be continued. Similarly, if you finally get up the courage to ask for sympathy but get none, it's easy to slide back into being passive and resentful.

If you're trying to become more sympathetic, or to become more assertive in asking for sympathy, you may find that you don't get much initial support or encouragement from your spouse. This may not seem reasonable, but I find that it often happens. You need to prepare yourself mentally for this. Others may not respond positively to your first offer of sympathy or to your first request for it.

If you want to become more sympathetic and to develop an ability to speak up about your needs, you must resolve to do more than just speak up once or twice. You must be prepared to con-

Imagine there are two magnets in your home. One pulls you in the direction of making your adult home "feel" like the home you grew up in as a child. The other magnet pulls your spouse to recreate their "at-home" feeling. Couples often blame each other for problems in their relationship, never realizing how they were "pulled" into recreating and reliving the antagonisms and tensions of their childhood homes.

tinue speaking assertively, even if you don't get much support or encouragement. You must have faith that others will respond if you give them time to adjust.

A well-known adage about changing behavior says, "Feelings follow actions." The first step is to begin acting sympathetically toward others and asking for the sympathy that you need for yourself. Expect everyone to be a little uncomfortable with this change at first. Eventually, your sympathetic actions and assertive requests will become a natural part of who you are. You, and those around you, will gradually come to feel at home with the sympathetic person you have become.

The Kid with a Peashooter

In his book, *Pain and Pretending*, Rich Buhler makes an analogy that gives me chills every time I think of it. He asks the reader to imagine an eight-year-old girl going down the street on roller skates. Suddenly she falls and cuts herself badly and starts to cry. Most adults would not hesitate to comfort her sympathetically.

Buhler then asks us to consider another eight-year-old girl. She, too, is on roller skates, but this girl shoots you with a peashooter and calls you a name as she zooms by. Most adults either would want to hit this girl or, at the very least, stay far away from her.

Buhler's point is that both girls may be in pain—different kinds of pain—but pain nonetheless. He suggests that we need to look beyond the way people show their pain if we want to act more sympathetically. Obviously, that can be hard to do.

If someone is attacking you verbally, being critical or sarcastic, it's difficult to feel sympathetic toward them. It's hard to think of the attacker as a person in pain who may be lashing out at the world in general, like a kid with a peashooter. Most of us get into fighting back, trying to exchange hurt for hurt.

Looking beyond the peashooter is an important step in learning not to use the peashooter ourselves when we're in pain, and in learning how to express our feelings with words of explanation and with tears. When we do this, it's easier for others to see our

Some adults show their pain with a "peashooter." They may call others names, put them down, or blast them with sarcasm. It's hard to be sympathetic to someone who shows pain in such ways. When children use "peashooters" to show pain, adults need to look beyond the child's unpleasant behaviors and seek ways to give needed comfort. When adults use emotional "peashooters," it's appropriate to confront them and encourage them to express their needs and pain in more appropriate, less harmful, ways.

pain as pain and to react sympathetically to it. When we lash out, others just fight back.

Low Self-Esteem

Low self-esteem makes it hard either to give or to receive sympathy. If you have little sense of self-worth, it may be hard for you to state your needs assertively or to withstand the countermoves of others. You'll have difficulty accepting your spouse's needs and requests for sympathy. You may become defensive and withdraw when your partner asks for sympathy or you may attack verbally if you view his or her requests as personal criticisms. A person with low self-esteem may be afraid to admit losing a job, a contest, or even a game for fear that others will think less of them. He or she may lie or invent elaborate excuses to avoid facing the truth.

If you are to give sympathy to others or receive it from them, you may have to increase your self-esteem. There are many good books available to help you know yourself better and value yourself more. Some of my favorites include Dorothy Briggs' *Celebrate Yourself*, Gary Smalley and John Trent's *The Blessing*, Matthew McKay and Patrick Fanning's *Self-Esteem*, and Nathaniel Branden's *How to Raise Your Self-Esteem*. In my book, *Dragon Slaying for Parents*, there's also a chapter that discusses some specific ways to improve self-esteem.

When Both the Husband and Wife Are Unsympathetic

When both partners in a marriage have trouble giving and receiving sympathy, it can be especially difficult to change the relationship. Even if one spouse works on learning how to request sympathy, the other almost certainly will be unable to give it. It's hard to keep making requests when one never gets a response. In such cases, the partners are likely to give up trying. The marriage then will lapse into old, unhealthy patterns. If you find yourself in such a situation, seeking help from a professional counselor may be the only way to make progress.

But It's Uncomfortable!

When you begin to change any behavior, you'll experience an initial period of discomfort. Change is frightening because it requires leaving the known and moving into the unfamiliar. Accept that this is normal. Everyone experiences it when they try to act in new and different ways.

What's important is to avoid letting self-consciousness and discomfort make you give up. Continue to work for positive change. Accept that you'll feel comfortable with the changes only after they've had time to become natural parts of who you are.

The process is something like getting a new pair of shoes. When you first wear new shoes, they often pinch and chafe. To break them in, you start by wearing them only for a short time each day. Gradually, as they become more comfortable, you can wear them for longer and longer periods. Soon they feel great and you wear them all the time. It will be like that as you practice new ways of giving sympathy and experience receiving it. Although it may be uncomfortable at first, before long it will feel great!

Points To Ponder:

1. Which points in this chapter are most relevant to you? Discuss them with your spouse.
2. Read at least one other book suggested in this chapter that talks about your special interests and needs.
3. What specific things in your marriage make it hard for you to become more sympathetic or to get your spouse to act more sympathetically?

Chapter 8

Why Is Lack of Sympathy a Two-Edged Sword?

The Doctor is a movie worth seeing if you're interested in sympathy. In it, William Hurt plays a crude, sarcastic, and unsympathetic doctor. When he becomes ill himself, he experiences personally how it feels to be in the hands of uncaring medical personnel. Despite the fact that he's suffering, he's unable, or unwilling, to accept any sympathy from his wife. At one point she says to him, "You've kept me at a distance; you wouldn't let me get close to you."

The doctor survives his ordeal, but thanks to his experiences as a patient, he becomes more sympathetic to those he treats. His experiences also teach him how to accept sympathy at home, and his relationship with his wife improves dramatically.

I find the plot accurate and realistic. People who have trouble being sympathetic also have a hard time accepting sympathy. In addition, they often make it hard for others to feel sympathetic toward them. They may hide their feelings or not discuss them at all. They may flatly refuse to discuss painful situations or disappointments. They even may be downright rude when simply asked how they're feeling.

In my office hangs a Bible verse that my mother once stitched for me: “You can’t heal a wound by saying it’s not there.” When one buries feelings, they usually are buried alive—they come back to haunt you. The lack of sympathy is a “two-edged sword.” It cuts not only those unable to receive sympathy, but also those who don’t receive sympathy when they need it.

There are many life experiences in which sympathy is the only thing that can help. Though it’s possible to recover from hurts without sympathy, it takes longer and healing never may be completed.

Chapter 9
Sympathy Questionaire

This questionnaire is intended only to serve as a guide for discussion. It's not a standardized test and it's not infallible. What it can do is help you focus on areas where you or your spouse need to become more sympathetic.

Answer the questions twice. Start by answering all the questions from your own point of view. When you are done, go back and answer the same questions in terms of how you see your spouse. For example, change how you think about question one from "Do *you* think about what your spouse or close friends are doing during the day?" to "Do you think your spouse thinks about what you or other close friends are doing during the day?" Be as objective as possible. Answer all questions "Yes" or "No."

	SELF	SPOUSE
1. Do you think about what your spouse or close friends are doing during the day?	Y N	Y N

	SELF	SPOUSE
2. Are you a forgiving person by nature?	Y N	Y N
3. Can you put yourself in another's place?	Y N	Y N
4. Do you think that it's necessary to apologize verbally if you hurt someone's feelings?	Y N	Y N
5. Are you quick to sense how other people feel?	Y N	Y N
6. Do you do things to help others who are not feeling well?	Y N	Y N
7. Do you feel compassion for those who are weak?	Y N	Y N
8. Are you sensitive to the needs and feelings of family members when they are ill?	Y N	Y N
9. Are you quick to know when someone needs encouragement?	Y N	Y N
10. Are you a sympathetic listener when someone needs to talk?	Y N	Y N
11. Are you the type of person to whom others turn when they need help?	Y N	Y N

	SELF		SPOUSE	
12. Are you easily moved to pity?	Y	N	Y	N
13. Do you notify family members if you will be late?	Y	N	Y	N
14. Do you give attention and care when others hurt themselves?	Y	N	Y	N
15. Do you try to help others feel better when you notice they are feeling down?	Y	N	Y	N
16. Do you accept sympathy from others?	Y	N	Y	N
17. Do you tell family members when you are feeling sick, depressed, hurt, or discouraged?	Y	N	Y	N
18. Do you ask family members how their day was?	Y	N	Y	N
19. Are you slow to criticize others?	Y	N	Y	N
20. Do you try to compromise with others when you differ with them?	Y	N	Y	N

Total the number of "Yes" answers:

SELF: ____ SPOUSE: ____

Quite arbitrarily, I have assigned the following scores:

Yes Answers	
15 or more	Excellent
9 to 14	Good
0 to 8	Poor

If you scored in the "excellent" range, don't feel so smug that you put this book down. A good score doesn't necessarily mean that you know how to show sympathy to your loved ones in the ways that they need. In addition, you may be living or working with someone who isn't sympathetic. This book can help you learn to deal more effectively with them. It's also important to pass sympathetic traits on to your children. This book discusses how you can do that, too.

If you scored poorly, don't give up. Sympathy can be learned. It's a tool that's essential for positive and healthy relationships, and you can add it to your tool kit. Keep reading; start working. Your life will change for the better.

Chapter 10

What Does "Being Sympathetic to Yourself" Mean?

Earlier I mentioned that the lack of sympathy could be a two-edged sword. If you are unsympathetic to the needs of others, you also will have trouble letting others give sympathy to you. In addition, you probably won't give yourself much sympathy either.

Every day we parent ourselves. Some of us are critical, demanding parents while others have learned to be sympathetic, compassionate, and caring. How do you parent yourself?

Let's look at the transactional analysis model again.

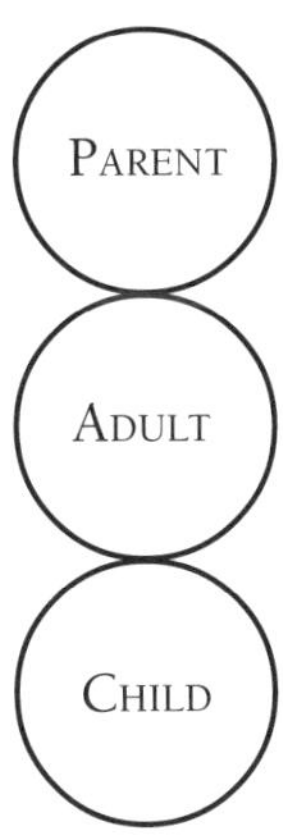

When you're tired, hurting, depressed, or discouraged, it's the CHILD in you that doesn't feel good. How do you treat your CHILD at such times?

Perhaps you say things like, "Quit complaining; you have it made," or "You can't relax; you need to work harder," or "You shouldn't be depressed; you have a great family." These are critical, unsympathetic ways of parenting.

A more sympathetic parent allows some time for relaxation after a busy schedule, accepts feelings, takes time off when sick, praises efforts, sets realistic goals, is patient with occasional setbacks and failures, doesn't criticize every mistake, rewards jobs that are well done, and honestly acknowledges problems by seeking medical help for physical ailments and counseling help for behavioral and emotional difficulties.

Sometimes the best way to become a more sympathetic parent to yourself is to detail specific new actions that you will take. How might you act as a more sympathetic parent to yourself? Make a list and refer to it often. This will help you parent yourself more sympathetically.

Like any other changing process, becoming a more nurturing parent to yourself may make you feel uncomfortable at first. Others around you may complain about the changes, too. They may even call you selfish. Don't give up. You gradually will grow more comfortable as you continue to parent yourself in positive and nurturing ways.

You can help make the changes permanent by looking into family of origin issues. Did your mother or father parent themselves in healthy, caring, sympathetic ways or did they ignore their own needs and feelings? Looking back will help you understand why you now act and feel as you do. It also will give you power to change the behaviors you want to change. Don't look back to find fault; look back to help yourself understand where some of your undesirable behavior patterns come from. Put another way, we don't look back to complain; we look back to explain.

I once saw a bumper sticker that read, "It's never too late to have a happy childhood." When I first read this, I didn't really understand it. I now realize what an important insight this is.

You may have been unhappy in your childhood home. That opportunity for a happy childhood is lost, of course. But this day, this moment, you can start treating yourself as the kind of parent for which every child longs. If you become a more nurturing, sympathetic, positive parent, a new opportunity for a happy childhood will unfold for you no matter what your age.

It's easy to describe the process of reparenting, but it can be very difficult to carry out. You should realize that it's a lifelong process. Know that you will backslide into negative parenting styles at times. Don't be discouraged. Renew your efforts and keep working to change.

You may recall that the term "codependent" is used to describe adults who grew up in dysfunctional families. Here they learned unhelpful behaviors and beliefs about how relationships work. In her book, *Codependent No More*, Melodie Beattie says that codependents often have characteristics that make it hard for them to give sympathy to themselves.

They try to please others instead of themselves. Because they feel safest when they're giving to others, they focus all their energy on other people and their problems. They feel that their own needs are less important than the needs of others. Often they don't know what they want, or they tell themselves that what they want isn't important. Because they feel unworthy and don't love themselves, they find themselves attracted to people with endless needs but little ability to give in return, people who sap their sympathetic energy.

Sound familiar? If you feel these statements describe you, or if you suspect that you are a codependent, I encourage you to do more reading. You'll learn why you have difficulty giving yourself sympathy. There are many books about codependency but two of my favorites are *Codependent, No More* and *Beyond Codependency* by Melodie Beattie.

Points To Ponder:

1. Were your parents nurturing and sympathetic to themselves? Discuss your answer.

2. In what ways have you been unsympathetic to yourself? Be specific.
3. In what ways could you become more nurturing and sympathetic to yourself? Pick one or two nurturing things to do for yourself each day. Do them.

Chapter 11

How Can I Become a More Sympathetic Person?

One of the first steps to take, and one of the most helpful things you can do, is to understand and accept how important it is to be sympathetic. This sounds simple but some people find it surprisingly difficult to believe that sympathy is necessary at all.

This is especially true if you grew up in a family whose members rarely showed sympathy toward each other. Then it can be very uncomfortable to consider the idea that sympathy is an essential part of good relationships. It even may seem unreasonable. If you find yourself feeling this way, try remembering past situations that were made more difficult because others gave you no sympathy.

A second step is to review your past to see how and why you missed learning to be sympathetic. As you do this, you also may be able to understand how lack of sympathy affected those around you as they attempted to deal with difficult and painful issues.

A third step is to start asking people who may be hurting what you can do for them. Ask your spouse or loved one how you can comfort him or her. If they are vague or don't seem to know, try paraphrasing or reflecting what you think they are saying to you.

This approach is helpful when neither person knows exactly what's needed.

For example, when a person expresses feelings with a statement like, "I'm afraid of the dark," a sympathetic response would be, "I bet it's scary for you sometimes when it's dark." If your spouse complains, "I think my boss has it in for me," respond with, "It's tough when your boss isn't being fair."

Responding sympathetically to the feelings of others doesn't require any special talents or unusual gifts. Even so, it's surprising how hard it can be for people to give sympathy. Men tend to offer suggestions rather than simply accepting feelings. To a child fearing the darkness, a typical male response is, "Well, lock the door if you're afraid." To the wife complaining about her job such a man says, "Why don't you quit?"

If you're faced with someone who responds to your problems or pain with suggestions, it helps to make it clear that you aren't asking for solutions. Tell the other person in plain language that what you really need is for him or her simply to accept your feelings without trying to fix them or make them better. Later, perhaps, you may seek suggestions, but that can happen only after the other person has accepted and validated your feelings.

A woman told me how, in deep depression, she had said to her husband, "I don't think my parents ever loved me." His response, "That's not true; I remember when they bought you something special for your birthday," was not sympathetic. Although he was trying to be helpful, instead of validating her feelings, he denied them. His unsympathetic response added guilt to her feeling of being unloved.

Remember, feelings don't have to be right. They're there whether they're right or wrong. It's important to accept others' feelings and to avoid implying that they shouldn't feel that way.

Husbands and wives often have difficulty accepting each other's feelings. For example, if your spouse says that she feels you don't love her, you first need to accept that's how she feels. You don't have to agree with her feelings, but you do need to convey clearly that you accept that she feels unloved. Once you've done that, and it may take a lot of patient listening, you can ask her why she feels that way. This needs to be done in a way that helps you learn what you can do differently. It's important to avoid putting the other person in the position of having to prove that their feelings are right.

Another way to become more sympathetic is to ask your spouse or children, "What have I done lately to make you angry or sad?" When you do this, you're giving them permission to share their feelings with you. It's best to do this after you've had a good day and are emotionally ready to accept what they may tell you. It's more effective to give others permission to share their feelings with you when you're able to consider responses thoughtfully without becoming defensive. On the other hand, don't wait forever for the perfect moment. It's better to share feelings imperfectly than to leave them buried until they become bitter resentments that are difficult to resolve.

Another step you can take is to learn, and to practice, some specific sympathetic responses. In other words, make a shopping list of sympathetic ways to react in difficult situations. I'll suggest a few just to get you started, but I encourage you to add to this list as you work on becoming more sympathetic.

- Call your spouse or loved ones if you're going to be more than fifteen minutes late.
- Consult your spouse any time you're going to spend more than an agreed amount of money. Discuss a specific figure in advance.
- Find out from your wife and children what their "language of love" is. Make a list to help you remember the things that make them feel loved and special. Be sure to show love in their language and on a regular basis. Be alert to things your spouse or children say they would like. Surprise them!
- Ask your spouse how his or her day went. In the morning, ask what he or she will be doing and then later ask specifically how the activities, meetings, or events went.
- During the day try to visualize what your spouse is doing. Imagine how he or she will be feeling when you see him or her later. Try to put yourself in their shoes.

- Send a card of encouragement or sympathy if your spouse has experienced a recent disappointment or simply needs encouragement.
- Accompany your spouse to funerals. Even though you may not be feeling the pain as they are, such sympathetic action helps your loved one feel that you care.
- Let others know of your plans in advance. Involve them in your planning. Don't start Saturday morning with, "See you at 3:00; I'm going golfing." During the early part of the week discuss what you'd like to do on Saturday. Try to reach an agreement so there are no surprises on the weekend. Work out a plan that considers everyone's needs.
- Try to compromise when you have disagreements with your spouse or children.
- Involve other family members in planning vacations and family outings.

Finally, remember that it may be necessary to act sympathetically before you begin to feel more sympathetic. Sometimes people think that they have to feel sympathetic before they can act that way. You may be surprised to find that acting sympathetically, whether you feel that way or not, causes you to feel more sympathetic. It's a natural response to the way you're acting.

It's easier to act your way into a better way of feeling than to feel your way into a better way of acting. Trust me; it works.

Points To Ponder:

1. Write out a sympathetic response to:
    - "You love my little brother more than me!"
    - "You never think of my needs." (from a spouse)
2. List some actions that you will take to become more sympathetic.

Chapter 12

What Should I Do If I Have Trouble Accepting Sympathy?

A man in counseling once asked me, "What should I do? I'm not used to getting sympathy. When I was a child, I just dealt with things by myself. I'd either go to my room or go for a walk."

I was at a loss for words. I rarely hear that question asked so clearly and directly.

An important first step is completing family of origin work around the issue of sympathy. You need to review and reevaluate your past to understand why you act as you now do.

Some people find the following exercise helps them to understand their present behavior. Remembering your childhood, complete these two sentences: "I was good when . . . " and "I was unable to . . . " For example, "I was good when I never complained"; "I was good when I went along with the program"; "I was good when I did what my parents told me to do without question." Or, "I was unable to share feelings"; "I was unable to express my opinions"; "I was unable to cry."

This exercise will help you see why you may handle pain by keeping it in. It will help you discover why you may have trouble asking for or accepting sympathy when painful things happen. It also will help you identify some childish strategies that you developed to manage pain.

Even when you've done some family of origin work, you still may have difficulty changing the way you act. I find that the phrase, "Face it, trace it, erase it, and replace it," provides a helpful outline of the steps needed to change behavior.

First, face it. Acknowledge that not giving, accepting, or expecting sympathy is a problem in your life. This step identifies the harmful ways that you now use to handle pain. Next, trace it. Follow these harmful behaviors back to their beginnings in your childhood. You will gain understanding about what motivates your present actions. Finally, erase it. This step involves replacing your present ways of handling pain with more useful, healthier ways.

As a child you may have kept your feelings in and developed physical problems. Perhaps you escaped problems temporarily by reading, playing sports, or watching TV for long hours. Perhaps you abused drugs, alcohol, or food. You simply may have pretended that your circumstances weren't so bad. This leads to a second part of the changing process.

You need to be able to express your feelings honestly before you can expect to receive sympathy from others. This can be difficult if years of childhood programming taught you to hold in feelings. It also can be scary. It helps to list "feeling words" that can give you labels for your feelings.

When I teach marriage classes, I hand out a two-page list of feeling words. I've included this list as an appendix to this book. People often are surprised to learn how many words there are to describe how they feel.

When people use anger instead of words to express their pain, it can be hard for others to hear the pain part of the message. They're more likely to hear only the anger. Sympathy is an unlikely response to anger. When we use anger to express pain, most people just want to avoid us. Worse, they may choose to fight back. At the very least, they're likely to become defensive. When any of these things happen, others have stopped listening to our needs and started taking care of their own. Our needs won't get met.

On the other hand, when we express our pain with feeling words like "left out," "trapped," or "unwanted," it's easier for others to hear, to accept, and to respond in positive ways. When we handle pain calmly, and reveal our feelings honestly, it's a lot easier for others to hear what we need and to give us sympathetic support.

Beyond simply expressing needs with words, getting the kind of sympathy you want requires learning how be specific. You have to let others know when all you want is a good listener who will accept your feelings and won't try to fix them. On the other hand, if you're truly seeking suggestions, you need to express that clearly as well. No one can read your mind, and no one knows what you need better than you do.

A common problem occurs when people first attempt to express feelings and ask for sympathy. Because they're inexperienced in being sympathetic themselves, they often pick bad moments, asking to have their needs met when their spouse is in a down mood, angry, or unresponsive for personal reasons. In counseling, people often tell of this happening. Remember, just because you're working on communicating your feelings doesn't mean that your spouse will be ready to hear you the first time you speak up. That's why you need to do more than just identify your feelings and express your needs. You need to continue being assertive even if you don't get an immediate positive reaction.

The moment you pick to ask for sympathy may not be the best time. That doesn't make your request unreasonable or your spouse a bad person if he or she doesn't respond the way you'd hoped. Don't give up. Come back at another time and express your feelings and needs again. Again, I recommend the book, *The Dance Of Anger*, by Harriet Lerner, to help you learn to express your feelings and needs and to deal effectively with others' responses.

Breaking old habits can be difficult. Sometimes it's stressful to express feelings, and it can be stressful to hear them. It's a little like a car in a deep rut. As it tries to move away from the rut, it often slips back. It takes times, practice, and some failures to get far enough away from the rut to avoid slipping back into it.

The struggle is worth it. The consequences of not making the effort can be deadly to people and to relationships. Just as cars stuck in ruts may be headed for disaster, so too are rut-bound marriages and relationships.

Points To Ponder:

1. What childish strategy or strategies did you learn as a child to help you manage pain and disappointments?
2. Take some time to explore and think about your feelings. Work to express these feelings in words.

Chapter 13

My Spouse Says I'm Not Sympathetic; I Think I Am. Who's Right?

This question often comes up during counseling. So, what's the answer? Of course, your spouse may be right, but you also could be an essentially sympathetic person who has trouble giving others the kind of sympathy they need.

For example, remember how we said that some people, especially men, feel that they're being sympathetic when they offer suggestions or solutions to problems? Unfortunately, this may not be what others really want. Often, when people are struggling with problems, they don't want, or even need, suggestions. What they want first is to have their feelings understood and accepted.

Perhaps you feel that you're being sympathetic when you tell someone to stop worrying about a problem. I remember a mother who described an incident with her seven-year-old son.

One morning he woke up complaining loudly about his unruly hair. First, she tried telling him not to worry about it. "No one cares about your hair," she said. When that didn't work, she tried unsuccessfully to fix it. In the end, her son left for school angry

People who have trouble giving sympathy to others often have trouble giving it to themselves. This man is driving himself to complete a job under a blazing sun. If this man could treat himself more sympathetically, he might put this job off till later in the day.

and embarrassed. The mother felt angry, too, because her son had rejected her sympathy. Both might have come away feeling better if this mother had used some sympathetic words that accepted and acknowledged how her child felt. She might have said, "I bet it's hard to go to school when you don't feel good about the way you look."

Sympathetic words accept and acknowledge feelings. They admit their existence without trying to judge whether they're right or wrong. This is what I mean when I say you need to accept another person's feelings.

Accepting feelings is especially important when someone thinks you're being unsympathetic. It's difficult, but important, to avoid becoming defensive at such times. Instead, show sympathy by asking them what they expected, or ask what it is that you're doing that makes them feel you aren't sympathetic. Listen closely, and you'll learn what their specific sympathy needs are. When you know exactly what others want, it's easier to behave in ways they experience as sympathetic.

A common mistake that many people make is offering advice to others rather than simply listening to their feelings, accepting them, and being sympathetic. If you want advice, ask for it; if you want someone simply to listen, then tell them that's what you want.

Another possibility is that you are being sympathetic but your spouse is not used to getting sympathy. He or she may misinterpret your actions. If low self-esteem is a problem for your spouse, such misinterpretation becomes even more likely.

I remember counseling with a man who told how he had cleaned the kitchen thinking that he was being helpful and sympathetic to

This man feels that he's being sympathetic by bringing his wife some ice cream when she is sick. It's a thoughtful gesture. Unfortunately, what his wife really wants is chicken soup. The ice cream makes her nauseous. It's important to pay attention to others' "language of sympathy," and to give what they really want and need, not what we think they should want and need. If in doubt, ask!

his wife. Unfortunately, she took it as a criticism of her housekeeping skills and became quite hurt and angry. Another man told of taking his children to the park. He thought he was giving his wife a break; she later accused him of "escaping the house." It's not always easy or simple to give sympathy.

As children, many adults learned to be sympathetic to people outside their homes, but they may not have learned to be sympathetic to those in their own families. This is one reason a person may feel that they are sympathetic, but their spouse may not agree; all the sympathy may be going to others.

Another issue comes up because some children are taught only to be concerned about the needs and feelings of others. They never learn to take care of their own emotional needs. They may grow up acting as if others' needs always are more important than their own. When they marry, such people tend to expect their spouses also to sacrifice everything for others willingly. They may put all their sympathetic energy into meeting the needs of people outside their families, spending endless time on jobs or working for causes. While such people sometimes perform useful work that truly benefits others, a terrible price may be exacted from their marriages and families.

I have counseled with many adults who were very sympathetic to people outside their family, but who did not extend this sympathy to those within it. Usually, they thought of themselves as sympathetic people, but their own family members never experienced much sympathy for their pains, frustrations, and disappointments. If a person's life and marriage are to be healthy, sympathy must begin at home.

Points To Ponder:

1. Ask your spouse and children what they would like from you when they're sick or disappointed. Talk about this when everyone is relaxed and feeling well.
2. Have you been more sympathetic to those outside your family than to those in it? If you said yes, give some specific examples. Think about what might be causing you to act this way. Discuss your answer with your spouse.
3. If you're really brave, ask your spouse or children to give you some specific examples of where you didn't act sympathetically. Not only will this help you learn what you need to do differently, it will help other family members let go of resentments that may be keeping them from seeking sympathy.
4. If your spouse hasn't been sympathetic to you, ask if you can share some specific examples with him or her.

Chapter 14

How Do I Teach My Children to be Sympathetic?

A parent once asked me, "Isn't sympathy caught rather than taught?" She seemed to be implying that if children hang around long enough in a sympathetic environment, they'd automatically learn to be sympathetic. While there is some truth in this idea, my response was an instinctive and vehement "No!" It's quite risky to assume that children magically will catch the ability to be sympathetic. Being sympathetic is something that most people learn to do only through specific teaching.

Don't get me wrong, some children seem to be more instinctively sympathetic than others are. Such children appear to have an innate sympathy for those in pain. However, most parents will need to make a conscious and conscientious effort to teach their children how to be sympathetic.

There are many ways to do this. I'll list a few here. As you read these ideas, ask yourself if your parents used any of these approaches. Doing this will help you understand why you may or may not have learned to be sympathetic.

Some parents feel guilty when they read suggestions like these. They worry that they haven't done all the things listed with their children. They may become immobilized with feelings of guilt. If you find yourself feeling guilty, consider this thought, "Don't let guilt keep you from doing what's right. It's never too late to do what's right."

Everyone enters adulthood missing some tools needed to make relationships work. Your children aren't the first. Even if they are grown and gone, it's not too late to tell your children about skills they might have missed learning from you. Let them profit from your experience.

I once counseled with a woman about her need to be more sympathetic. Eventually, she met with her grown children and openly discussed how her lack of sympathy had kept her from giving them this important tool. It must have been awkward to admit, but she may have spared them considerable grief. Although she was late in teaching her children about sympathy, she did the right thing when she could. She saved her children from learning the way she did—the hard way.

Single parents can have special difficulty in teaching their children to be sympathetic. They lack the support of another parent to reinforce their efforts. Also, youngsters in single parent homes may not have opportunities to observe one parent being sympathetic to the other. If you are a single parent, you need to recognize this obstacle and be sure to employ many of the following suggestions.

Some techniques to use for teaching sympathy to your children:

1. Model sympathy

Being a positive role model is important and has a powerful impact on children's behavior.

- Do you ask your spouse how his or her day was?
- Do you show an interest in his or her work?
- Do you take the time to call if you know you'll be late?
- Do you offer to do things for your spouse when he or she is sick, or feeling down, or simply to lighten his or her load?
- Do you show concern for the misfortunes and illnesses of neighbors or friends?

When you act sympathetically, it's important to call your children's attention to what you're doing. Most parents know the importance of being a good model for their children. One way to reinforce this modeling is to talk specifically about how to give sympathy. Don't just wait and hope that your children will notice and understand what they're seeing. Be more direct. For example, say, "Mrs. Jones down the street is sick, so I'm going to take her some dinner," or "Mom's had a hard day. Let's all pitch in and clean the house."

As children, people learn how to be sympathetic (or how not to be) by watching their parents interact. Obviously, this boy has had some unfortunate lessons. When he grows up, his spouse, his children, his friends and co-workers will feel the effects of his lack of sympathy and he will pay the price.

2. Assign chores

Chores teach responsibility and accountability. They also build self-esteem and teach sympathy. Many parents underestimate the importance of having their children complete regularly-assigned chores.

In my family, we have always assigned chores to our children. We display the chores on a chart to help the children remember their responsibilities and to help us avoid nagging. Read my book, *Dragon Slaying For Parents*, if you want more information about chore charts. We always have used an allowance system, as well. Getting an allowance helps children learn the value of money and how to budget. It also teaches children that they can make things happen. They don't have to be completely dependent on their parents. Parents also must point out the significance of reliably completing chores, not leaving them for others.

Doing chores responsibly is a way of being sympathetic to other members of the family. Say things like, "Your mother works hard for the family and she needs your help in making your bed," or "Your dad has worked hard this week for the family; you can help him by mowing the lawn."

Some parents do everything for their youngsters because they felt overburdened with chores as children. They do too much, thinking that they're showing love. This prevents children learning to think and consider the needs and feelings of others. They come to believe it's the job of others to take care of them.

3. Reward sympathetic acts and penalize unsympathetic acts

Children learn sympathy through the effective use of reward and by suffering consequences for disobedience or unsympathetic acts. Consequences have a place in teaching sympathy, but it's essential to avoid focusing exclusively on them. Then children learn that only misbehaviors attract attention. It's true that consequences can be effective when used sparingly.

For example, if your youngster barges noisily into the house while someone lies ill in bed, a few minutes of grounding may be appropriate. Such a consequence emphasizes the importance of considering the needs of others. Nothing teaches sympathy better than praise. Rewarding children's positive behaviors is vital. Let your child know through praise when they've acted sympathetically. Praise that specifies the desired behavior is best. For example, say, "Thanks for setting the table for dinner; that really helps me a lot."

4. Let your children know if you're not feeling well

Many parents seem to feel that it's important to hide their feelings or misfortunes from their children. Actually, you need to tell your children when you're sick or disappointed. Give them the opportunity to be sympathetic to you. Tell them what you'd like them to do. Remember, if you're sick or depressed, your actions probably will show it anyway. You may yell or withdraw and your children will feel that they are the cause of your unhappiness. It's better to label your actions. Inform others specifically about why you're acting the way you are.

I once counseled with an author. As I can attest, being rejected is a fact of life in the book publishing business. This man never discussed his hopes and disappointments with his children. They only heard about the books that got published. He gave them no opportunity to understand his moods or give him sympathy for his less-than-happy publishing experiences. He wasn't teaching them how to be sympathetic. He wasn't even modeling hard work to achieve a goal. His children never knew the real extent of his efforts.

In contrast, when I tried to publish my first book, I purposefully told my children about the many rejections I was receiving. This allowed them to be sympathetic and kept them from feeling guilty or responsible when I was down. It also modeled persistence in reaching a goal. Let your youngsters know about your disappointments, trials, and sadness. Give them the opportunity to learn how to be sympathetic.

5. Help your child consider the feelings of others

For example, don't allow your children to take only two or three party invitations to their school classes and neglect the feelings of the other kids.

I remember an incident that happened when I was coaching a soccer team. Before a game, one of my players brought two invitations to a Halloween party for friends on the team. Fortunately, I intercepted him and told him that I would keep the cards until after the game when he could pass them out quietly. Imagine the effect on team spirit that giving the invitations before the game would have had. Treating teammates sympathetically is an important part of successful team play.

My daughter was invited to a birthday party where she had a great time. As she left, she happened to see five sleeping bags in the hallway. You guessed it: five of the girls were spending the night, but my daughter wasn't invited to the slumber party. Her good time and happy feelings were dashed by an unsympathetic display of favoritism.

Don't allow your children to make fun of siblings or classmates in school. Help them understand why others might act as they do. Help them to be sympathetic to the other person's needs, problems, and point of view.

6. Don't give endlessly without receiving

Some parents continue to do and do for their youngsters, although their children are unhelpful around the house. These parents seem to believe that their children will learn to do things for them if only they can do enough for their youngsters.

Unfortunately, this method teaches many children only how to be selfish. Also, your resentments will grow if you continue to do for children who give no cooperation in return. This is not the basis for a healthy relationship. If your youngster is uncooperative around the house, it may be necessary for you to say something like, "No, I won't do that; because you said no to me when I asked you to ______________. I don't like doing this, but I'm not going to do things for you if you won't consider and respond to my needs." You'll be amazed at how quickly your youngster will start paying attention to your needs if you assertively stick to this approach.

7. Watch TV shows together

Many sitcoms get their humor from showing people making cruel fun of one another. They show and glamorize people who are not sympathetic to others. As you watch shows with your child, be sure to point out examples of sympathy and examples where adults and children are not sympathetic. Consider eliminating certain shows from those you allow your children to watch if you feel that the content is not healthy.

This man is not only being sympathetic to his wife, he's teaching his children how to be sympathetic adults. These children will grow up knowing how to give, and how to receive, sympathy.

8. Buying presents or cards

Help your children remember to buy cards and presents for your spouse and for their brothers and sisters on special holidays and birthdays. Children need more assistance and guidance in this area than parents think. Help them think of the needs and interests of others, and encourage them to save some of their own money for cards and gifts.

9. COMMUNITY INVOLVEMENT ACTIVITIES HELP TO TEACH SYMPATHY

There are many community activities that will help your youngsters learn sympathy. For example:

- For years our church has prepared meals once a month for needy families. When our children were little, my wife would take them with her to help serve the families and prepare the food.
- We have sponsored a child in Costa Rica for many years and our children have been aware of this. We could have reinforced this even more by having the children each donate a small amount of their allowance every week. It was a special thrill for all of us to see the boy we sponsored during a recent mission trip to Costa Rica.
- Our community has had a walk for the hungry for many years. Youngsters and adults obtain pledges from people and walk to earn money for the hungry of the community and the world.
- Collect toys that your youngsters have outgrown or have them pick some of their toys to give to Goodwill or to a fire station for needy children. A client told me one of her Christmas traditions was to give her four-year-old son ten dollars and have him buy several toys at a toy store. They then took the toys to a nearby fire station to be given to needy children.
- Have your children donate a portion of their allowance to the church you attend.
- This one definitely is not for everyone, but when our children were younger we had three different foster children live with us for short periods. This experience helped our children to appreciate the difficulties other children experience.
- Our family adopted a grandfather when our children were young. My wife had taken food to a man while his wife was in the hospital dying of cancer. For many months after that, we invited "Grandpa Al" to our house for dinner and some holidays. Although Al never had any children of his own, he was always very patient with our children.

- All our children have participated in short mission trips to Mexico with their high school church youth group. During their trips they helped to build small houses for less fortunate people.
- Be assertive in teaching your children what to do if they have a friend who is sick or in the hospital. Encourage them to visit the hospital or to send a card.

Points To Ponder:

1. List several ways that you will begin to teach your child to be more sympathetic.
2. Discuss ways that your parents helped you to become sympathetic.

Chapter 15

How Do I Handle Unsympathetic People

Every day we encounter people outside our families, at work, or in the general community, who are not sympathetic to our needs and feelings. Although this book focuses mostly on intimate family relationships, a few words about handling unsympathetic people might be helpful.

We've all experienced them:

- The X-ray technician who says, "Oh, my! I'll need to take another picture of that!" and then refuses to tell you why.
- The boss who won't let you take a certain week off to be with your family on vacation or who gets upset when you're out sick.
- The doctor who doesn't bother to explain why he thinks you need to have "some additional tests."
- The teacher who sends home only negative comments about your child.
- The fast food clerk who rudely asks you to repeat your order or who says it was all your fault when the order gets messed up.
- The mechanic who forgets to order the part you need.

There are so many situations like this that it's impossible to give specific suggestions about each and every one, but some general comment may be helpful.

I'm sure by now, you're well aware why some people are not sympathetic. Usually they simply never learned how. No matter what people's profession is, no matter how much education they have, if no one teaches them how to be sympathetic, they won't be. Look back at chapter 6 on "What Should I Do if My Spouse Is Not Sympathetic?" This will give you some insights on dealing with unsympathetic people in general. The first step is always to maintain a rational perception about why another person may be acting unsympathetically. If you look at his or her lack of sympathy as something purposefully withheld from you, or if you feel that everyone should be sympathetic, you are setting yourself up to feel stressed, angry, and crazy. It actually helps to try to feel sympathy for the other person's needs or the situation in which they must exist. Try to imagine the pressures and stresses with which he or she lives. When you are able to look at situations in a healthy, rational manner, you will be more able to remain peaceful even when you are treated unsympathetically.

After you have mastered the ability to stay calm in the face of unsympathetic behavior, you'll need to kick in the assertiveness skills. It's essential that you speak up and express your needs, sympathetically, but firmly.

Don't expect the other person simply to roll over and reply, "Oh, you're so right! I'm truly sorry that I wasn't sympathetic to your needs." This would be wishful thinking carried to extremes, I'm afraid. Don't get me wrong, some unusual people may respond to you just that way. More often, though, expect the other person to make angry countermoves. Don't be alarmed by these. Simply anticipate them and prepare yourself to repeat your feelings and restate your needs, calmly and firmly, for as long as it takes.

Another technique is to write a short note to the unsympathetic person. State your feelings, what led to those feelings, and what you would like from that person in the future. Writing a note is not a cop-out. It lets you get out all your thoughts in a positive

Parents often do and do for their children, hoping that they will learn to be sympathetic from the example. But sympathy is a two-way street. Sometimes it's okay to refuse children's requests, especially when they have not pulled their weight in the family or shown sympathy for others. This kind of firm fairness helps children learn and understand more about what sympathy really is.

manner. It also allows the reader time to review your comments before they have to respond. This avoids catching people off guard with assertiveness and helps them escape the trap of becoming defensive and hostile.

If the person continues to act unsympathetically, you may have to decide whether it's worth quitting your job, getting a new doctor, or taking your business elsewhere. Sometimes, there's no choice but to acknowledge the sad truth that some people simply have no sympathy to give. They are empty, crippled individuals who are better avoided.

Please don't load your guns and go out looking for a fight today as you interact with people. You don't have to abandon your own sympathetic nature in order to deal with those who lack sympathy. In fact, sympathy is essential in these situations. Simply prepare yourself to handle unsympathetic treatment from others constructively and sympathetically.

Chapter 16

Is It Hard to Be Sympathetic Sometimes?

Definitely! I've coached youth soccer for many years. I'm easily sympathetic when a child is hurt during a game. In fact, I often run out to comfort a youngster even before the referee gives me permission to enter the field. This gets me in trouble with referees, but I find the impulse to care for a child hurt in the line of duty irresistible. On the other hand, if the same child is hurt horsing around before the game, I'm likely to be a lot less sympathetic. It's a stretch for me to muster up sympathy for people who get hurt doing things they've been told not to do.

People often have trouble being sympathetic in such situations. Perhaps you've just warned your children not to jump on the beds. No sooner do you leave the room than they ignore you and jump on a bed. Of course, someone ends up falling off and getting hurt. Or there's the times when you've told your husband to stay home from work because he's sick. He goes anyway, and, of course, becomes sicker.

Or you've told someone not to take on an extra duty; they've already got too much to do. Later she complains about how overwhelmed she is. The fact that she has this problem because she ignored your good advice makes it doubly hard to listen sympathetically.

Then there's the friend with the lousy boss. You've repeatedly advised this person to look for work elsewhere. It's an effort to accept his feelings and remain sympathetic as he goes on, day after day, doing nothing but endless complaining.

We need to remember that it's times like these when sympathy may be especially important. In addition to any actual hurt, the other person often is feeling guilty, foolish, and embarrassed. Though it's hard to fight the temptation to say, "I told you so," this is the moment to make a conscious effort—a choice—to be compassionate. It will be an effort, but you must make the choice, and the effort, to give sympathy.

When someone gets hurt, it's fairly easy to recognize and respond to his or her need for sympathy. However, what happens when both people in a relationship are hurt at the same time by an event? Sometimes I describe such situations using a word picture.

Suppose two people are driving down the street in their car. Without warning, they are hit by another vehicle. Both receive severe, multiple injuries. Because both are injured, it can be very difficult, almost impossible, for them to be sympathetic to each other's injuries. They're hurting too badly themselves.

Situations like this happen all the time in real life. Both parents may find themselves grieving the loss of a child who has left for college, or been seriously and permanently injured, or has died. Both partners in a marriage can be terribly affected when one unexpectedly becomes unemployed. Such situations often arise. At these times, it's important to realize that two injured people can't take care of each other. Hopefully, others will see the need and reach out in sympathy. If not, the partners must seek out appropriate counseling on their own, so that both can be helped through the difficult time. Remember, if two people are badly injured, they don't usually set each other's broken bones. They get help from a doctor. Emotional hurts may require outside assistance, too.

It also can be hard to give sympathy to someone who shows his pain in ways that tend to push you away. If someone is hurting, and he shows that hurt by criticizing you, by yelling at you, or by blaming you, it can be very difficult to remain compassionate. High self-esteem will help you avoid becoming defensive in such situations. Try to remember that most people never learned how to ask for sympathy when they are hurting. They may be hurting so badly that they're unable to act sensibly. You may need to say, "I know that you're really hurting, but it's hard for me to want to comfort you when you show your pain in that way (yelling, blaming, criticizing)." Don't count on them immediately changing their behavior. They may need some time alone to think and get control before they can approach you, and their pain, in a healthier way.

When a loved one, or a friend, has been experiencing difficulties for a long time, it often is hard to remain sympathetic. It's difficult to keep listening patiently and remain supportive when someone has been out of a job, or ill, or injured for months or years. This is especially true if the other person's situation has negatively affected your life in some way. Don't make things worse by demanding sainthood of yourself. Being sympathetic doesn't mean that you should let yourself be used for a doormat. Your support can take the form of encouraging your friend or loved one to take some specific action to overcome their problem.

It's even okay to express your disappointment or frustration occasionally if he or she doesn't seem to be taking corrective steps. After all, you have feelings too, and you can express them in loving, supportive ways. The person who is suffering needs you to be there, but often they are so absorbed in their struggles that there is little sympathy for what you may be going through. If you are to maintain the emotional reserves you need to be sympathetic, you may have to go elsewhere to get some support for yourself—to a supportive friend or counselor, for example. Take care of yourself. Make sure your own sympathy batteries get recharged!

It can be especially difficult to be sympathetic toward someone who has hurt you. Perhaps you are asking why you should even try to be sympathetic in such a case. To answer that question, let's think about some situations that can arise.

You may have had parents who were not there for you when you were growing up. Perhaps they hurt you physically, emotionally, or sexually. Maybe one of your parents hurt the other in such ways or deserted the family. Friends and children can "drop the ball," or take actions that hurt or disappoint you.

It's completely true to say that developing compassion for the person who hurt you is not the first thing you need to do in such cases. To heal yourself from this kind of hurt, you will first need to acknowledge that you were hurt. You will need to explore the hurt and describe it to yourself, a good friend, or a trusted counselor. Writing a letter to the person who hurt you (but not sending it), also can be an effective way to "get the poison out" so that healing can begin. These steps take time.

At the appropriate moment, putting yourself in the shoes of the person who hurt you, attempting to be sympathetic to him or her, can help you to move on. When you develop compassion for someone who has hurt you, then you will find there is less and less room for anger. Carrying anger around is like having to carry a backpack full of heavy bricks. It takes all your energy.

I remember one man who told me during counseling how he had forgiven his father for his abusive upbringing, because he knew his father's childhood was no better and he had done the best he could. This same man, however, said he could not forgive his mother because he felt she deliberately meant to hurt him. This man was choosing to carry a backpack full of bricks. Though he was not ready to acknowledge it, his mother's childhood experiences deserved compassion, too. He would never be able to put the backpack of anger down and rest until he could see the world sympathetically through her eyes as well as his own.

Remember, there are many situations in life where it can be hard to be sympathetic. Sometimes, giving sympathy will require you to exert a tremendous effort. You may need to renew your commitment to that effort, day after day, over long periods of time. It may not be easy, but your success can help others through difficult times, and free you from resentments that chain you to the past, and keep you from moving on into a new, and better, present. Sympathy is your key to freedom.

Chapter 17
Some Personal Stories

In my counseling practice, I've discussed the issue of sympathy with hundreds of adults, teenagers, and children. Because sympathy is a tool that many people lack, it's a topic that almost always comes up sooner or later.

When Raising Children

A married man with three young children once shared some thoughts with me about his personal struggle to become more sympathetic. I'd like to pass these along now.

"In our home I always felt that asking for, or expecting, sympathy was a selfish and weak thing to do. I don't think my parents intentionally taught that, but I caught it.

"I wanted to please my father and I knew he expected us to be tough, to endure pain without complaint, to get over disappointments quickly, and to work hard. My pain never seemed bad enough to excuse me from this code or to receive sympathy.

"Dad expected Mom to keep house and never showed that he cared if her workload became overbearing. He would make large purchases, like a new television or a camera, without consulting her. He rarely took us out to eat because he felt that dinner with four boys in a restaurant was too chaotic. For similar reasons he refused to take us on long vacations. One year Mom drove us by herself a thousand miles to Denver because Dad wouldn't go. On Saturday mornings he hustled us out of bed early and kept us away from television with warnings against laziness. I felt guilty if I didn't get all the chores done and done well.

"My father was never cruel or abusive. He spent time with us in home projects, Boy Scouts, the PTA, and sports programs. I wanted to please him, and when he criticized me more than encouraged me, I felt defeated. I tried to hide my mistakes and show Dad only the positive things I did. I never got the positive reward I expected, like an encouraging word. He never told me he loved me, never praised me, never offered to talk about my problems, and never appeared to feel sorry for me.

"Sometimes, though, my father surprised us with sympathy. One time I fell off the top of our clubhouse, about eight feet down to the ground, on my back. My head missed a concrete slab by inches. It knocked the wind out of me and I was scared. Dad ran over when he saw me fall and I expected him to yell at me for falling or to tell me I wasn't really hurt that bad. Instead he comforted me and seemed surprised that I didn't get hurt worse.

"Mom offered compassion and encouragement sometimes, but she was busy sympathizing with my three brothers who, unlike me, knew how to ask for sympathy. I was the good boy and everything seemed fine with me, so the attention went to my brothers who externalized their problems and feelings while I kept mine inside. I never asked my father or mother for sympathy; I just waited for it to come.

"I remember one time when we went out for ice cream; everybody got a cone except me. I didn't like the cone part and I reasoned to myself that my parents wouldn't buy me anything different, so I just said I didn't want anything. I felt afraid to say what I really wanted, so I just cried while everyone else ate their ice cream.

"I learned to feel sorry for myself over long walks and one-way conversations with my dog. I never told my dreams or my problems to anyone but God. From my father I learned that any such confessions showed weakness. More than that, I learned that revealing my weakness would result in rejection, for my father appeared to reject me when I was weak.

"I learned to hide my weaknesses, to cover my mistakes. If I had a problem, I fixed it myself, alone, sometimes at high personal expense.

"It's still hard for me to let someone know that I'm hurting or that I have a need. My family isn't sure when I need sympathy because I cover up my feelings and needs. I'm afraid that if I express them, my family will reject me like I feared my dad would. When people offer sympathy, it's hard for me to receive it.

"When I was in junior high, my grandfather died. A girl came up to me at church and said, "I'm sorry to hear about your grandfather." I shrugged it off; told her I was fine, and walked away feeling embarrassed. At the funeral I asked my aunt why so many people were crying. I didn't think people should cry so much.

"Recently my mother-in-law had heart surgery and my wife went to be with her for a week. Church members offered meals, childcare, and other help, but most of it I turned down. I wanted to prove to my wife and everyone else that I could take care of our children and house by myself.

"As a child, I learned how to get my own needs met outside the home. Other people seemed much more sympathetic than my family, and I fell in love with anyone who gave me sympathetic attention. I still do—especially if that person offers compassion without me revealing any of my inner needs.

"I find it hard to be sympathetic to my children when they're sick or hurt. Like my father, I minimize their pain and expect my children to show adult self-control and tolerance. Becoming aware of my childhood experience has helped me to change my reactions to my children's requests for sympathy.

"The other night my seven-year-old son, who whines often, complained about a light scratch on his ankle. I wanted to repeat all those things my father used to say, "It's nothing. I can't even see it. Don't be such a whiner." Fortunately, I caught myself. I sat down with him and said something like, "I bet it hurts. Is anything else wrong?"

"We started talking about some other events in his day that had upset him. I honestly thought reacting with sympathy would make my children wimps. Now I think it's helping us all to communicate better, to feel better about ourselves, and to learn how to express our feelings clearly."

When Tragedy Strikes

"I never really thought I was an unsympathetic person until I was forced to take a good look at what being sympathetic really means.

"I thought I was a kind and caring person, but found that I was never taught the skills of being sympathetic. It's something I'm working on now. I am finding that even small gestures can make a big difference in how a person feels.

"Two years ago, my sixteen-year-old son died. I was overwhelmed by the outreach of sympathy from family, friends, and acquaintances. I was greatly touched to get letters from people I didn't even know offering prayers and support. It made a profound difference in my life and helped me through a devastating experience.

"I am working hard now to give back some of that sympathy to the people I know. I find that our relationships are strengthened.

"My husband and I are very near to the empty nest time now. I find myself looking forward to our time together. I feel a renewal of our relationship through small gestures we practice. It's almost like we're dating again for the first time. A single red rose on my bedroom pillow can make me feel good for days.

"I have found that sympathy is not a skill that is easily acquired. It requires time and effort, but this book has been a good guide, leading me to understand the power of sympathy."

A Last Word

Stories like this reveal the power of sympathy, the lost aspect of love. Start now to bring more sympathy into your life. More love, joy, and happiness will follow. We wish them all to you and yours.

Feedback for the Authors

We would appreciate your taking time to complete this short questionnaire. It will help us revise and improve this book. In addition, your experiences will help others who are struggling with the same problems you have faced. Without your written permission, we won't disclose your name or attach it to any comments you make. Thanks for taking the time to complete this.

1. What section or sections were most helpful to you? Why were they helpful?

____

____

2 What sections or paragraphs were unclear to you? __________

____

____

3. Describe why they were unclear and make any suggestions that you feel may help clarify the material: ________________

____

____

4. Share any personal stories about sympathy that you feel we might want to add to this book. Tell us the section in which you feel your material best fits. For additional space use reverse or attach an extra sheet.

____

____

____

5. Write two or three sentences on how the book helped you and how you think it might help others.________________________

____

6. Additional comments:

____

____

____

Name: ______________________________(Optional)

Phone Number: (___)____________________(Optional)

Return This Form To: Tom Prinz and Reed Elliott
3585 Maple St., Suite 288
Ventura, CA 93003
(805) 644-5490

Bibliography

Beattie, Melody. Codependent, No More. Hazeldon Publications, 1987.

Beattie, Melody. Beyond Codependency. Hazeldon Publications, 1989

Bloomfield, Harold. Making Peace With Your Parents. New York: Ballanti Books, 1983.

Branden, Nathaniel. How To Raise Your Self-Esteem. New York: Bantam Books, 1987.

Buhler, Rich. Pain and Pretending. Nashville, Tennessee: Thomas Nelson Publishers, 1988.

Conway, Jim. Men In Midlife Crisis. Elgin, Illinois: David C. Cook Publishing Co., 1978.

Conway, Sally. You and Your Husband's Midlife Crisis. Elgin, Illinois: David C. Cook Publishing Co., 1980.

Conway, Jim and Conway, Sally. Women In Midlife Crisis. Wheaton, Illinois: Tyndale House Publishers, Inc., 1984.

Briggs, Dorothy. Celebrate Your Self. Garden City, New York: Doubleday & Company, Inc., 1977.

Ellis, Albert and Harper, Robert. A New Guide To Rational Living. North Hollywood, California: Wilshire Book Company, 1961.

Larsen, Earnie and Larsen Hegarty, Carol. Days of Healing, Days of Joy. Hazelden Foundation, 1987.

Lerner, Harriet. The Dance of Anger. New York: Harper and Row Publishers, 1985.

McKay, Matthew and Fanning, Patrick. Self-Esteem. Oakland, California: New Harbinger Publications, 1987.

Missildine, W. Hugh. Your Inner Child of the Past. New York: Pocket Books, 1963.

Prinz, Tom. Dragon Slaying for Parents. Lancaster, Pennsylvania: Starburst Publishers, 1992.

Prinz, Tom. Dragon Slaying for Couples. Tempe, Arizona: Blue Bird Publishing, 1995.

Simon, Sidney and Simon, Suzanne. Forgiveness. New York: Warner Books, 1990.

Smalley, Gary and Trent, John. The Blessing. Nashville, Tennessee: Thomas Nelson Publishers, 1986.

Stoop, David. Making Peace With Your Father. Wheaton, Illinois: Tyndale House Publications, Inc., 1992.

Stoop, David. Living With a Perfectionist. Nashville, Tennessee: Thomas Nelson Publishers, 1987.

Wright, Norm. Making Peace With Your Past. New Jersey: Fleming H. Revell Co., 1985.

Wright, Norm. Marital Counseling. Denver, Colorado: Christian Marriage Enrichment, 1981.

Appendix

FEELING WORDS

abandoned
accepted
adequate
affectionate
afraid
angry
annoyed
anxious
apathetic
apprehensive
ashamed
had
betrayed
bitter
bottled up
broken up
caged
caring
challenged
cheated
cherished
cooperative
cornered
crazy
deceived
defeated
defensive
deflated
degraded
dejected
dependent
depressed
deprived
deserted
despair
desolate
destroyed
disappointed
discontented
discouraged
disgusted
disorganized
doubtful
drained
embarrassed
emotional
empty
enraged
envious
exasperated
exposed
falling apart
fearful
foolish
forgiving
forsaken
frantic
frightened
frustrated
furious
genuine
giving
glad
happy
hassled
hate
helpless
hemmed in
hesitant
hostile
humiliated
hurt
hysterical
ignored
immature
impatient
impotent
incompetent
incomplete
indifferent
infuriated
inhibited
insecure
insignificant

cold
competent
complaining
confused
jealous
judged
left out
lonely
loving
loyal
mad
mean
melancholy
miserable
mixed up
mournful
mystified
nasty
nervous
obnoxious
obsessed
offended
open
on edge
out of control
outraged
overburdened
overwhelmed
dissatisfied
distressed
distrustful
dominated
pain
panic
paralyzed
persecuted
pessimistic
petrified
pleased
powerless
prejudged
pressured
proud
pulled apart
put down
puzzled
quarrelsome
rattled
reasonable
rebellious
rejected
repulsed
resentful
responsible
restless
revengeful
gloomy
grief
grouchy
guilty
robbed
sad
sarcastic
secure
selfish
serious
shaky
shattered
sickened
skeptical
small
smothered
sorrowful
sorry
squelched
stubborn
stupid
submissive
suffocated
suspicious
sympathetic
tense
terrible
terrified
insulted
intimate
irked
irritated
threatened
timid
touchy
turned on
uncertain
uncomfortable
uneasy
unhappy
unimportant
unsettled
unstable
upset
uptight
used
valued
violent
vulnerable
warm
wasted
weak
withdrawn
wonderful
worried
worthless

To order additional copies of:

The Lost Aspect of Love

send $9.99 plus $3.95 shipping and handling to:

Books, Etc.
PO Box 1406
Mukilteo, WA 98275

or have your credit card ready and call:

(800) 917-BOOK

Other Books by Tom Prinz

Dragon Slaying for Couples: Strengthen and Enrich Your Marriage by Dealing with Hidden Issues, published in 1995. This book presents all the tools necessary to maintain a healthy marriage or to enrich a marriage. Most importantly it also covers the 'dragons' or hidden factors that will prevent a couple from applying the tools effectively and consistently. Cost $15.00 plus $3.00 for shipping.

Dragon Slaying for Parents: Removing the Excess Baggage So You Can Be the Parent You Want to Be, published in 1992. Most parenting books present tools or strategies for being an effective parent. Few books have addressed the hidden factors or 'dragons' as Tom has labeled them that will interfere with one's ability to apply the parenting tools. 'Dragons' also cause parents to become too angry or too emotional when dealing with their youngsters. Cost $13.00 plus $3.00 shipping and handling.

The "Dragon" portion of this book is also available in Spanish.

To obtain copies of these books write to Tom at:

Tom Prinz, M.S.
3585 Maple St., Ste. 288
Ventura, CA. 93003

or call (805) 644-5490

To Inquire About Author Appearances and/or to set up a seminar for your group contact Tom at the same address and phone number.

Special Bargain

Order *both* books for only $20.00, plus $5.00 for shipping.